INTERNET
SAFETY

Keeping you and your family safe while using the internet

J Pagden & D Moran

2017

The information provided within this book is for general informational purposes only. While we try to keep the information up-to-date and correct, there are no representations or warranties, express or implied, about the completeness, accuracy, reliability, suitability or availability with respect to the information, products, services, or related graphics contained in this book for any purpose. Any use of this information is at your own risk.

Although the authors have made every effort to ensure that the information in this book was correct at press time, the authors do not assume and hereby disclaim any liability to any party for any loss, damage, or disruption caused by errors or omissions, whether such errors or omissions result from negligence, accident, or any other cause.

MY WIFI ROUTER DETAILS
(enter your Wifi router details here)

Make	
Model	
Serial Number	
Wifi Network Name	
Wifi Password	
Admin Login User Name	
Admin Login Password	

TABLE OF CONTENTS

INTRODUCTION

This book is addressed to parents. Parents of children who use the Internet and its many and varied systems.

We have a major problem as parents in this digital age. It is not a simple problem, and it's not a problem that has been faced by previous generations. It can be summed up as follows:

- **Our children know more about technology than we do!** If, like most parents, your phone misbehaves in some way, you'll probably ask your kids to fix it rather than head over to the nearest tech shop.

- **Technology is developing at such a rate that we simply cannot keep up!** There is no shame in admitting that we cannot keep up with technological development. Thousands of apps are released each day; new smart phones are released monthly and new gadgets and devices come onto the market that, to previous generations, would have been considered "magic"! No single person can keep up with it all!

- **The big technology companies do NOT have our children's wellbeing at the core of their business!** It is a natural feature of the capitalist society that we live it, that companies are motivated by profit. They will do anything within the law to maximise sales of their products. Tech companies are not looking after our best interests – but theirs.

- **Undoubtedly the Internet is a great resource. Criminals use the Internet as often as any other user.** It is said that that around 70% of burglaries are researched on the Internet prior to being carried out. The Internet hasn't created new criminals, it is being used by criminals to further their own ends.

- **We as parents feel inadequate which makes us fearful of everything our children are up to**. This feeling of inadequacy should be an excuse. We need to step up to the mark and become a little more knowledgeable so that

1

we are better able to care for our children. Knowledge allows us to keep our children safe.

This book is designed to provide parents with a resource for understanding the issues that we face. It should also be a 'go-to' resource when technical and non-technical advice is required.

We hope that you find it helpful.

J Pagden & D Moran
Galway, 2017

1 THE INTERNET - WHAT IS IT?

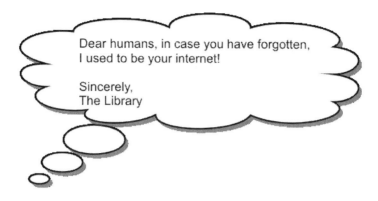

For the past 4 years, I have delivered Cyberbullying and Internet Safety talks to children in schools across Ireland – from 8 to 18 years old. Often, I ask my audience what the Internet is. I have had 2 instances where a young person has been able to answer the question accurately. Mostly, I'm told:

"It's a place you can look up stuff"
"It's a place you can chat to people"
"It's a place you can get bullied"
"It's a place you can play games"
and on and on…

While all of these answers are entirely accurate - they do not tell us what the Internet actually *is*. They are a list of what can be done on technologies that use the Internet.

In the absence of a correct answer to *what* the Internet is, I then ask *where* the Internet is!

"It's on your phone"
"It's in the Wifi box"
"It's in satellites"
and then my favourite…
"It's everywhere", to which I would then look out of a window and actively look for the Internet outside!

To be fair to the youngsters, parents, teachers and educators, who are asked the same two questions, mostly give me blank expressions - most adults are as clueless about the Internet as the children!

The point of this preamble is that this thing called the Internet has become so much a part of everyday life, that we all simply take it for granted. If you are born after the late 1980s, early 1990s, and most particularly if you are born in the 21st century, then the Internet predates you and you simply accept it as 'being there', almost like the air that we breath. However, a little understanding of the nature of the Internet is important for 'grounding' the rest of this book.

So - what exactly is the Internet? I'm not going to bore you with historical facts and figures - if you are interested, then use your favourite search engine and search for "what is the Internet" - all your questions will be answered! However, for my purposes, the concept of the Internet first got a mention as far back as 1962 - when J.C.R. Licklider of MIT wrote a series of memos documenting his "Galactic Network" concept. His vision was a globally-connected set of computers - over which one could quickly access information and programs from any location on earth.

In 1965, an MIT researcher, Lawrence G. Roberts, successfully connected two computers together using telephone lines - creating the first ever wide area network thus demonstrating that Licklider's idea was feasible. This was followed in 1967 when Roberts, his work on interconnected computers, referred to the network as "ARPANET". When eventually built this became the first version of the Internet.

During the early days of this innovation, ARPANET was so costly, that only academics and the military were able to afford to use it. However, as we all know, this did not remain the case, with the Internet now being used by approximately 4 billion people across the world. In layperson's terms, the Internet is simply a large collection of computers that are connected together using various networking technologies. To be clear, we are talking here about the *physical* infrastructure - NOT the things that use the Internet. The World Wide Web - is *not* the Internet - it is a communication system that *uses* the Internet. Likewise, email *uses* the Internet; SnapChat *uses* the internet; YouTube delivers its content *over* the Internet and so on.

It is probably worth noting here that there are two 'flavours' of the Internet. The first is what I call the "Internet of Screens". This is the Internet that we have grown to love and adore – it is so called because we use screen-based technologies to access the Internet - our laptops have, computers and our mobile devices all have screens. The second is what academics are calling the "Internet of Things" (or "IoT"). This is where non-screen-based devices are being connected to the Internet. Jacob Morgan, Forbes.com 2014 says: "Simply put, this is the concept of basically connecting any device with an on and off switch to the Internet (and/or to each other). This includes everything from cell phones, coffee makers, washing machines, headphones, lamps, wearable devices and almost anything else you can think of.

This also applies to components of machines, for example a jet engine of an airplane or the drill of an oil rig".

The Internet is simply incredible in its concept, and in its power to deliver information, knowledge and entertainment, joy, pleasure. It has revolutionised the way we communicate with one another and is changing the very fabric of human society. There is no denying that it is wonderful, and has massive potential for good. However, we ignore the possible negative effects of innovation - to our detriment.

2 CYBER BULLYING

Chinese Proverb: May your life someday be as awesome as you pretend it is on Facebook!

"Deindividuation" is a word used by psychologists to refer to what happens to social norms when a person's identity is concealed - in other words, what do people get up to when they are guaranteed total anonymity. According to the theory of deindividuation, someone who is an anonymous member of a mob is more likely to act violently toward say a police officer, than a person whose identity is known.

The question to ask is this – 'What would I do if I was guaranteed total anonymity?'. As W. Belle puts it: "…when we are anonymous, we no longer have any of the constraints we would normally feel with other people: no morality, no decency, and no rules at all. At that point, it is merely our own moral compass which guides us as to whether we do something or not.".

This sense of total anonymity is exactly what people get when they go on line. There is no correlation between the person's real-life persona, and their behaviour while being anonymous on the Internet. In fact, the shy, retiring child, who wouldn't say 'boo' to anyone in class, can often be completely emboldened while on the Internet - simply because of the perceived anonymity.

I mentioned the "moral compass" above - another phenomenon that we perhaps take

for granted. What is a moral compass? Simply put, it is the inner voice that tells a person what direction they should go when they are faced with decisions involving right and wrong. But the issue is, not everyone shares the same moral compass! And when that person is given the freedom of anonymity on the Internet, their moral compass might easily 'permit' them to engage in behaviours that are completely at odds with society's norms.

Let's look at some of these online behaviours – i.e. the most common forms of Cyberbullying:

1) **Harassment**: Repeatedly sending offensive, rude and insulting messages to a person.
2) **Denigration**: Distributing information about a person that is derogatory. This includes written messages and images (including digitally altered images).
3) **Flaming**: Online 'fighting' using messaging systems. There are frequently what are referred to as "flame wars" - where individuals engage in a protracted attack against each other.
4) **Impersonation**: Creating a fake Social Media account (or indeed any other type of online account) in the name of your victim, and then using that account to post vicious or embarrassing material to or about others.
5) **Doxing (or Outing)**: Tricking an individual into revealing real-life, personal information, and then publishing this information to public forums, opening the individual up to online abuse and/or very real danger.
6) **Trolling**: Deliberately provoking a reaction from people by saying offensive things. "The most essential part of trolling is convincing your victim that either a) you truly believe in what you are saying, no matter how outrageous, or b) you give your victim malicious instructions, under the guise of help. Trolling requires deceiving; any trolling that doesn't involve deceiving someone isn't trolling at all; it's just stupid. As such, your victim must not know that you are trolling; if he does, you are an unsuccessful troll."
7) **Cyberstalking**: Where the communication systems of the Internet are used to pursue, harass or contact another person in an unsolicited fashion.

There are a few facts that you need to be aware of:

1) Bullying, by definition, needs to be **repeated**. A once-off vicious comment does not constitute bullying. We are only human after all and sometimes we say things we don't mean. It is only bullying if the act is repeated.

2) Bullying always represents an **imbalance of power**. It is always Big versus Small; Strong versus Weak or a Group versus an Individual.

3) Owing to the anonymity so readily available on the Internet, **ANYONE** can be a bully. Most parents find it hard to accept that their child could be a bully! In fact, it is one of the hardest things we parents must do - admit that our children are not always perfect!

According to Allan L. Beane:

4) **Girl bullies**:
   a) are more likely to bully other girls although may bully weaker boys
   b) engage in group bullying more than boys
   c) seek to inflict psychological pain on their victims
   d) often appear as 'angels' around adults while hiding their cruelty
   e) frequently target their victims through accusations of sexual activity
   f) attack within close-knit 'networks' of friends

5) **Boy bullies**:
   a) tend to be more physical (tripping, spitting, hitting, pushing)
   b) attack victims verbally about race and sexual orientation
   c) physically target smaller and weaker individuals
   d) engage in sexual harassment
   e) engage in extortion and blackmail.

Later, we'll talk a bit about what to do if your child is actually bullying someone, here are some practical steps that you and your child can do to protect yourselves against cyber bullies. Note, these steps can be age dependant and need to be tailored to your own circumstances.

As a parent:

1) Always be aware of what your children are doing online. In this day and age, it is no longer okay to simply abandon your child to the Internet. You need to know a couple of things about their activity. Firstly, know the apps they are using. If you don't understand what a particular app actually does, you need to research it. We have an entire chapter on the typical apps that kids are using. However, technological innovation is so fast that you really need to do your own research.

2) Children fear a few things when it comes to the Internet. Highest on this list is their fear of your over-reaction. Never over-react if your child comes to you for help about Cyberbullying (or any issue on the Internet). If you do over-react - you risk losing the most precious thing you have - your child's trust and your lines of communication with your children. I cannot emphasise this enough - you MUST keep talking to your kids! If that means biting your tongue then so be it. And most importantly - do not play the blame game - kids don't intentionally become victims - it's almost always as a result of errors of judgement - after-all - they're kids!

As a victim of bullying:

1) **Never reply to a bully**: Bullies are motivated by many different needs and emotions: envy, arrogance, narcissism, shame, fear, inadequacy, or a need to boost self-esteem. Putting it very simply, bullying makes the bully feel better. All bullies need to know that they are having an impact - real life bullies can see the impact of their actions. Cyber bullies cannot see the impact of their actions, so they crave some sort of response. If your child is being bullied - the last thing you want to do is reply to the bully. A reply is telling them that they are getting through to you. Bullies do not care how their victims reply - be it politely or with venom - as long as they get a reply.

> For every action, there is an equal and opposite reaction, plus a social media overreaction.

2) **Never "Like" or "Dislike" bullying behaviour**: You have often watched scenes in movies and on television where physical bullies get a crowd of onlookers egging them on. The equivalent behaviour on the Internet are the 'comments'; 'likes'; 'retweets'; 'follows'; 'views' etc. that are the hallmark of Social Media interaction. Bullies want a crowd, and in Social

Media terminology, 'liking' bullying comments is the online equivalent. It is very easy to read a negative comment as being a joke, or see an embarrassing image of someone as being hilarious. Unless you know the full context of the message, you cannot know if your involvement is contributing to a much more serious bullying situation than not. Your child should stay away from any of the nasty messages that they will inevitably come across on the internet.

3) **Keep evidence**: I'm often ask how to do this - it's simple, take screen shots. Your kids will know how to do this - but if not, simply search for instructions on the Internet. If the authorities (the police or similar) get involved, then they will want to see the evidence.

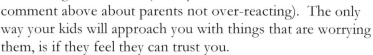

4) **Report it**: You must encourage your children to report ANYTHING that makes them feel uncomfortable when using the Internet (see my comment above about parents not over-reacting). The only way your kids will approach you with things that are worrying them, is if they feel they can trust you.

There are three ways of reporting bullying:

    a) Your child should be happy enough to report everything to you the **Parent**.

    b) Most jurisdictions in the world have an official online facility for young people to report things that are disturbing them, in a safe and sometimes anonymous environment. In Ireland, the website to report it to is **www.hotline.ie**.

    c) Depending on the jurisdiction you live in, the **policing**

authority will provide varying degrees of support for victims of Cyberbullying. Again, in the Links chapter you'll find contact details of many such authorities.

5) **Block people**: All Social Media technologies and all multiplayer games provide ways for users to 'block' unwanted behaviours from other users (the word "block" is a generic term and different systems have different terms that they use). A quick and relatively easy way for your child to protect themselves from harassment, is to 'block' the offending person. Again, as the parent, once you are familiar with the apps and games your child is using, you can research how to block offensive behaviour.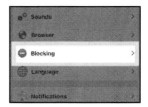

6) **Change your own account**: There is one major problem with the mechanism of 'blocking' a person… on the Internet you cannot block a human - you can only block an account, and there is little to stop Cyber Bullies from setting up multiple accounts. If your child is persistently bullied having already blocked an offensive account, it is possible that the bully is simply setting new accounts, and reconnecting with your child and continuing with the bullying. In this case, it might now be time to change your child's account in some way.

This will depend on the system you are dealing with. Some systems allow free name changes; other systems require you to pay for a change; others will require you to set up a new account, while others ban the use of multiple accounts. Again, you'll need to do your research on the apps and games your kids are using.

Safety Tip#1: For each of the apps your kids use, search the Internet for instructions of how to change their account if they are persistently bullied or harassed.

3 THE SOCIAL MEDIA PLATFORMS YOUR KIDS ARE USING

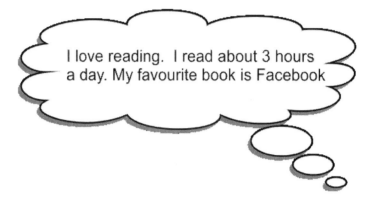

I love reading. I read about 3 hours a day. My favourite book is Facebook

According to Merriam-Webster, Social Media is defined as:

"forms of electronic communication...through which users create online communities to share information, ideas, personal messages, and other content..."

Any online system that facilitates people getting together to communicate with each other and share content, in social groupings, will fall under the umbrella of Social Media. This includes the systems we automatically associate with Social Media - like Facebook, SnapChat and Instagram, but also includes systems like YouTube and most modern multiplayer games like Clash of Clans, Road Blocks and many others. In this chapter, we are going to examine the Social Media platforms (Apps, Websites or Games) that children are currently using and look at the dangers each system presents and provide you with useful, practical information on how to manage each system.

First, some statistics:

Social Media Websites

Name	Monthly Visitors
Facebook	2,000,000,000
YouTube	1,000,000,000
Instagram	700,000,000
Twitter	313,000,000
Reddit	250,000,000
Vine Camera	200,000,000
Pinterest	150,000,000
Ask.fm	160,000,000
Tumblr	115,000,000
Flickr	112,000,000
Google+	111,000,000
LinkedIn	106,000,000
VK	90,000,000
ClassMates	57,000,000
Meetup	30,300,000

Social Media Apps

Name	Monthly visitors
Messenger	1,200,000,000
WhatsApp	1,200,000,000
QQ Chat	899,000,000
WeChat	806,000,000
Instagram	700,000,000
QZone	652,000,000
Viber	249,000,000
LINE	218,000,000
Snapchat	200,000,000
YY	122,000,000

Despite murmurings of Facebook's demise, as you can see, the Facebook website outperforms its closest rival (YouTube) by a factor of two, and in terms of Apps, the Facebook Messenger app is joint top performer with WhatsApp. Given that both WhatsApp and Instagram are owned by Facebook, that effectively puts Facebook in a league of its own. I don't see Facebook going away anytime soon!

And even if your children no longer consider Facebook to be "cool", they are probably all using Facebook-owned systems without even knowing it.

A bit about Terms & Conditions

You retain ownership of what you put up on Snapchat (Snapchat TOS, 2014)

But you also give them a licence to basically do what they want aside from claiming ownership (Snapchat TOS, 2014)

How many user agreements have you accepted in your life without reading them? It's probably one for every online account you've ever set up (email accounts, social media accounts, shopping accounts, bank accounts etc), every bit of software you've ever used and every gadget you've bought. You've probably agreed to literally thousands of pages of dense, unread (unreadable?), legal jargon in your life. You've signed away your soul!

I'll let you decide whether these companies are trying to 'screw you over' or not. What I am saying is that these companies have unlimited money to hire the best legal teams on the planet, to ensure that they have the *right* to screw you over, and in the process, ensure that you can do nothing about it.

For example, if you publish an image to their system, they own the image! Okay, you and your family are having a fabulous time on vacation in the south of France. You decide to upload several pictures to your various online accounts (probably Facebook if you're over 25 years old...probably Instagram if you're under 25 years old) - those wonderful Social Media systems that allow instantaneous exhibitionism. After-all that's what Social Media is all about, isn't it? Social Media gives you the perfect way to share your precious memories with close friends and family members - right? Well, there's actually more to it than that! Don't be too shocked or surprised when you find your gorgeous face being used in an advertisement for erectile dysfunction! You might well ask, how could someone use your image like that? Well, because YOU GAVE THEM PERMISSION, by accepting their terms and conditions.

Very soon after Social Media was invented, some enterprising person realised that people's personal images amounted to an unlimited supply of content that could be exploited by advertisers. Hence, every Social Media system has a clause written into their Terms & Conditions that gives them the legal right to use your images commercially.

Typically, the conditions you signed up to state that you're granting these companies "worldwide, non-exclusive, royalty-free, sub-licensable and transferable license to use, reproduce or distribute" your private images. They do go to great pains to point out that you still 'own' the content - they are simply reserving the right to monetise your content - and will you see any of the revenue? - no!

So, just to be clear, deleting my images from my Social Media accounts is the way to go - I'll be safe, right? Hmmm...ah... no! There is almost always a clause in the Terms & Conditions that states the company can keep the rights to deleted images until a "commercially reasonable" time has passed.

You do have choices though - a simple choice really... you could choose to stop using Social Media! (Shock, gasp - how can the world see the food I'm about to eat?)

Currently, there are hundreds of things that we don't really need to buy anymore - so many things are downloadable - so what if it's against the law! One compelling reason for paying for a product is that if you buy something - you own it! If you walk into a shop and buy say a new microwave oven, the shop cannot change its mind a week later and ask for its return! But is this true for online purchases as well? Hmm, don't be too quick to assume so. If you had bothered to read the Terms & Conditions a little closer, you would have seen a lot of these companies have a section in their terms that states that they "reserve the right to change, suspend or fully remove" any product or content that they choose - and they are not referring to removing it from their site so that others cannot buy it, they are referring to the thing that you paid to install on your device.

Let's remind ourselves of something - Social Media companies are hugely motivated – they just don't have our best interests at heart - they are motivated by one thing and one thing only - the bottom line, and they will do anything within the law to generate profits, if that is at the expense of our safety and privacy - they don't care!

Let me be clear however, I am not suggesting that these companies are doing anything illegal, but I wonder sometimes, how 'honourable' they are. They rely a lot on the foolishness of humanity. They rely on the fact that as humans we do not read the Terms & Conditions. They rely on the fact that we NEVER bother researching apps before using them. We download an app mostly because we've heard about it from friends or family! There's a name for people like us - sheep! Social Media relies on humanity's sheep-like downloading habits. "It must be good because everyone is using it" - wrong. "It must be safe because it's made by Apple" - wrong. "It must be legit because it's Google after-all" – wrong (these statements might be true - it's the *assumption of truth* that I say is wrong). My best piece of advice when it comes to the next latest and greatest - is to hold back jumping on it with the rest of the sheep - for at least 6 months. After the 6 months do your research and only then decide whether or not to use it.

Understandably, I've painted a grim picture of Social Media so far. The remainder of this chapter is going to detail the good, the bad, the ugly and the how-tos of some of the Social Media platforms out there today. The list is provided in the order of importance according to the children and students that I get to meet in my talks.

DISCLAIMER REMINDER
The following information is accurate at the time of writing however, you must understand that with the pace of development of all technologies, references provided may become redundant.

SnapChat

When SnapChat was first brought to the public's attention, it quickly became known as the "Sexting App" owing to its 'disappearing messages'. It felt safe to send naked selfies to people, because they were deleted from the recipient's device after a few seconds. Well, times have moved on and SnapChat is no longer the App it used to be. For one, the features of the App have expanded exponentially. Snap Maps is the latest offering which provides a map of the location of all of your friends in real time - very scary. Secondly, SnapChat - just like the Tobacco companies before them, have learned to 'cover themselves' by providing guidance and assistance for staying safe. It is in their vested interest to protect the reputation of their App. So, SnapChat themselves give a lot of advice and information to do with safety.

Safety Tip #1: You as the parent, need to do some reading:
1. Firstly, dive into the SnapChat Safety Centre. This is a great resource, but please, please, please remain sceptical.
2. If you still have the energy dive now into the SnapChat Safety Tips and Resources. Here you'll find links to the SnapChat privacy policy, instructions on how to block people and information on Cyberbullying.

Safety Tip #2: Don't share your account login details with anyone. If you do, you are in effect giving control of your account to someone else - who then can use your account (under the guise of your name etc) to carry out any mischief they want.

What is a SnapChat 'streak'? Simply put, you are rewarded by SnapChat with a 'streak' if you send messages (and get receipts for those messages) to the same person on 3 or more consecutive days. It doesn't matter what is in those messages - a message containing a single full stop will suffice. 'Streaks' are designed to keep people coming back to SnapChat, and believe it or not, children are completely addicted to streaks. I have met children who have streaks of six, seven, eight hundred days! They will do ANYTHING to keep their streaks going. Do you ever wonder why your child is SO distraught when you take their phone off them? It's because they will lose their streaks if they don't keep them up!

But, our kids have worked out a way of NOT losing their streaks even when they lose their phones - they simply give their account details to someone else who then keeps their streaks going on their behalf. How many people have they given their account details to? Do they fully trust those people? Do they use one password for everything (most people do)? If this is the case their trusted friends now have access to all of their accounts. And here's the problem - when you are young, friendships are transient and fickle. The person you trusted yesterday with the SnapChat details, could well be a hated enemy today. Your enemy now has your details!

Parents, you need to talk to your kids about sharing details with anyone. It really is a big no-no.

Safety Tip #3: Make sure your kids are abiding by SnapChat's Community Guidelines which state that no one should send content over SnapChat that:
- is pornographic or sexually suggestive (especially when minors are involved)
- include drawings or captions that make something sexual - even as a joke
- is illegal
- is intentionally offensive, insulting, or threatening toward the recipient
- invades someone else's privacy
- deceives someone into thinking that you're somebody else
- depicts you or anyone else engaging in dangerous or harmful activity
- depicts any sort of illegal activity
- threatens any person's safety – even as a joke
- is an impersonation
- promotes terrorism
- could be considered hate speech

Safety Tip #4: During one of my talks I met the local priest who was talking to the primary school kids I was about to talk to. He mentioned an ancient Aramaic expression: "There are three things that you can never get back - the spoken word, a spent arrow, and a lost opportunity". I thought this was particularly relevant to our current SnapChat generation. Indeed, there are two immutable facts when it comes to communication on the Internet - one, once you click the send button, you can NEVER get the message, or picture back, and two, once you've click the send button, *someone else* is now in control of that information. So, safety tip number 4 is this:

Safety Tip #5: Use utter discretion when sending content on Snapchat. For primary school children, I like to refer to this a the "Granny Rule" or the "T Shirt Rule". Would you like Granny to see this image? Would you wear this message on the T Shirt and walk through town with it? If the answer to either question is "no" then the message should not be sent.

Safety Tip #6: Ensure that you have configured your SnapChat privacy settings so that *you* are in control of who views your content. Because settings are continuously changing it makes no sense to put definitive instructions here. However, SnapChat provides full instructions for adjusting settings on their support website. In summary, from the SnapChat privacy settings support site, you have several options:
- Who can contact me?
- Who can view my story?
- Who can see me in a quick add?

SnapChat also provide on the same page some vital things to remember:

"Even if you choose 'My Friends,' anyone you're in a Group with will be able to communicate with you"

"If you post a Snap to your Story, and then change your settings so only friends can see your Story, others may still be able to see the Snaps you posted before the change"

A noticeable absence from the SnapChat settings support page is any mention of Snap Maps settings! To find instructions on how to manage your Snap Map settings (and it is VITAL that you do this), go to the support page, click into the Search box under the SnapChat Support title, and enter "Snap Maps" as your search criteria. You will be given a set of results. Scroll down and click on the article entitled "Find your Friends on Snap Map". On this page, in the paragraph entitled "Tap on a friend to start a chat", you'll find a link to "Ghost Mode". This link takes you to the Snap Map location settings. My advice to all users of SnapChat is to set your account to Ghost Mode by default. Only very cautiously allow select friends to know your location.

Safety Tip #7: SnapChat is often used for bullying and abuse. If your child is victim of such abuse via SnapChat, they need to block the offending account and report the abuse to SnapChat. Instructions for blocking an account are provided by SnapChat in the support section. Instructions for reporting abusive content is provided in the I Need Help section of SnapChat support:

- browse to the "I Need Help" site of SnapChat (address provided below)
- click on "Report a safety concern"
- click on "A Snap or Chat I've received"
- depending on the nature of your concerns, click on one of the options: nudity; threat; bullying; illegal activity; undesirable content;
- Instructions will then be provided for how to address the issue.

On occasion, I have been given practical suggestions from audience members. Where appropriate I will include them in the book.

Audience Suggestion #1: One parent told me that she and her husband have one non-negotiable rule - they, the parents, have all of the children's credentials for all of their accounts - and the parents reserve the right to keep an eye on everything their kids are doing online. If the kids change a password without informing the parents, or if they set up a new account without giving the parent the credentials, this results in an automatic internet ban of some length.

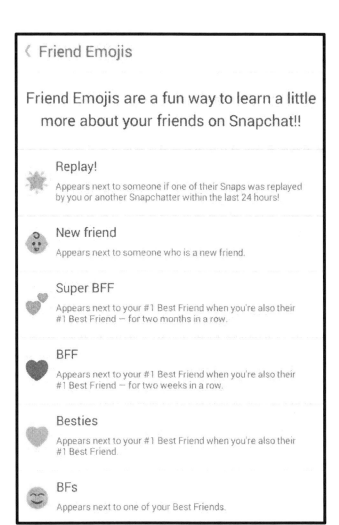

YouTube

 I've put YouTube second on the list, but I suppose it should really be top. Over the last 12 months, I have noticed the meteoric rise in popularity of YouTube amongst the young members of my audiences. Now, in primary schools, I'm finding virtually all 8, 9 and 10-year-olds are actively using YouTube for most of their entertainment. Indeed, around 30% of that age group now claim to have their own YouTube channel and claim to be posting their own videos. You might be surprised to know what kids of that age are watching. These are the top seven video categories that young kids are saying they are watching:

- "Vloggers" - a person who posts "Video Blogs" - or videos about their daily lives.
- "Let's Plays" - videos showing the game-play of a computer game.
- "Try Not To Laughs" - these are videos of people watching other videos. It's a competition where 5 or so individuals are videoed watching audience-submitted funny clips - the object of the game is to remain straight-faced for as long as possible. The winner of the game is 'last man standing'.
- "DIYs" - videos about how to do or make 'stuff'
- "Epic Fails" - videos of people falling mostly!
- Music videos - the number one source of music for young people.
- "Call Outs" - videos of individuals challenging their rivals to real-life fights.

Every kid now has their favourite Vlogger. If you're into playing Minecraft then you're probably into Stampylonghead (previously Stampylongnose). Stampylonghead is not only a Vlogger, he's also a "Let's Play" YouTuber who is most famous for his 2000+ published videos and his 8.6 million subscribers. His videos have been viewed 6.1 billion times!

If you're a teenage girl then you are almost certainly into Zoella -

fashion tips for teenagers - 300+ videos uploaded, 11 million subscribers.

Have you heard of these?

- "Danisnotonfire"
- "Romanatwoodvlogs"
- "AmazingPhil"
- "DailyGrace"
- "ShayCarl"
- "BFvsGF"
- "JacksGap"
- "ShaneDawsonTV"
- "Joey Graceffa"

They are all vloggers that kids have told me about. If you haven't heard of them, how can you possibly know whether their content is appropriate for your children?

You cannot remain ignorant of your child's YouTube activity. I met a 10-year-old in a large primary school recently. He proudly gave me his YouTube channel details. It was several weeks after I had met him that I found the time to look at his channel. When I last checked he had 113 videos published to his channel. He is a vlogger and to be honest, shows potential as a very talented vlogger. His videos are innocent commentaries on his interests. However, while I was looking down his video list a video caught my eye (for confidentiality reasons I am not going to name it). In this video, the boy was telling a heart-rending, very personal story. In it he couldn't contain his emotion. Either the incident he is referring to is true - in which case he should NOT be publishing it, or it's false and he is acting for the camera - in which case it is referred to as 'click-bait' - content designed to get people to click on it. Either way, I would be very surprised if his parents were aware of this video. In fact, looking at his videos, they all appear to be filmed in his bedroom - and nowhere is there any sign of an adult.

I'm not saying that having a YouTube channel is a bad thing - in fact it is an incredible tool for creativity and learning. It's just that you cannot allow your children to use YouTube unsupervised.

Safety Tip #1: NEVER allow your children to have unrestricted access and use of YouTube without supervision. In fact, get the Internet out of their bedrooms. It is when they are alone in their bedrooms that much of the nonsense we're talking about happens.

Safety Tip #2: Make sure that YouTube has "restricted mode" turned on. You can find up-to-date instructions and guidelines on all YouTube issues on their official Help Center page. Scroll to the bottom of the Help Center page and expand the "Legal, safety and copyright" tab. Click on "Policies, safety and reporting" link. On this page, you're going to find articles categorised into three columns: Policies, Reporting and Safety. Click on the "Privacy and safety settings" which you should find in the Safety Centre column. Click on "Disable or enable Restricted Mode" to get instructions.

Obviously, now that you've seen the topics in the YouTube Help centre, you should take a look as some of the other sections: "Protecting your Privacy"; "Child endangerment"; "Nudity and sexual content" etc.

Instagram

 If you ask children to tell you what Instagram is, they will often tell you it's "Facebook for kids" or "Mini-Facebook". You see, Facebook seems to be the only Social Media platform to which parents have actually, universally decided to restrict access. In my experience, very few kids in primary school have Facebook accounts - for two reasons: 1, parents have banned Facebook and 2, they don't need Facebook if they have Instagram. I wonder how many parents know what the implications of that are!

- In 2012 Instagram was acquired by Facebook.
- Just like most other Social Media platforms, Instagram cannot accept applications for accounts from children under the age of 13 years. However, the signup process is not authenticated, and children simply have to choose a birth year that makes them "of age". Whether your child has an Instagram account or not - is up to you as a parent - no one else is going to police it.
- By default, anyone can view your profile and posts on Instagram, meaning that unless your child has intentionally made changes to their settings, anyone can view the pictures that your child posts.
- If your child's account settings are not tightly controlled, anyone can comment on your child's images - and not everyone plays nice!
- It is easy to set up a fake Instagram account. During my tour of schools around Ireland, in almost every school I am told about the existence of fake Instagram accounts.
- When a digital image is taken on any device, various bits of information are hidden inside the image. Depending on the device, this might include the make and model of the device, the date and time the picture was taken and, if the devices location services are turned on, the longitude and latitude (the GPS coordinates) of the location of the picture. This 'hidden' information is called "metadata". If those pictures of your daughter at her birthday party are posted via Instagram on an

account which is set to public, and then geotagged as occurring at your home, your daughter's privacy has just been seriously compromised, and perhaps her safety as well.

- Many people on Instagram simply choose to ignore the Instagram Community Guidelines. If you're allowing your child unsupervised use of Instagram, they will inevitably stumble across inappropriate material.

Safety Tip #1: If you are not happy with allowing your child onto what is in effect a version of Facebook, and if you're not happy that to gain access they have to lie about their age, and if you're not happy that they will probably see inappropriate content - then, your responsibility is to say 'No' to your child!

Safety Tip #2: Ensure that location services is turned off for Instagram. You can turn off location services for Instagram through your phone settings. Or, you can do it on an image by image basis. Share your image as normal, but on the last page - the Sharing page, make sure that "Add location" is turned off.

Safety Tip #3: Block random followers and / or remove random followers. This is only an issue if your child's account is not set to private.

Safety Tip #4: Turn off commenting on posts. This is done on a post by post basis, and you can do it either prior to posting it, or after it has been posted. If you find that a post is attracting lots of negative comments, you can turn off commenting retrospectively, which will hide all comments so far made and prevent further commenting. Instructions for doing this are very clear on the Instagram website. On the Instagram help page, enter "comment" into the search box at the top of the page and press enter. Scroll down and click on the article entitled "How do I turn comments on or off for my posts".

Safety Tip #4: Don't be afraid to report abusive, inappropriate or illegal content. On the profile page of the offender there are options for both blocking and reporting them. Check out the relevant pages on the Instagram support site.

WhatsApp

WhatsApp was bought by Facebook in 2014 for $19 billion! Since the acquisition, WhatsApp has been unstoppable, boasting over a billion users each month and in 2015, Jan Koum was boasting over 30 billion messages sent through it PER DAY! Indeed, there are reports that now claim that there are more WhatsApp messages being sent, than ALL global SMS messages combined! I'm worried about this. Facebook pays a fortune for an App that is given away for free, has no ads and has no in-app purchases. One thing is certain - Facebook didn't fork over their cash out of some altruistic sense of charity! No, they see the potential for massive returns on investment! And they can only be hoping for an ROI if they know they have some way of monetising WhatsApp. One key to understanding how they intend to do this, is the announcement last year from WhatsApp, that they would be sharing our data and information with Facebook. This makes no sense though - as you all know (because WhatsApp tells you each time you start a new conversation) WhatsApp messages are encrypted: "Messages you send to this chat and calls are now secured with end-to-end encryption...". According to WhatsApp themselves "No one can see inside that message. Not cybercriminals. Not hackers. Not oppressive regimes. Not even us.". Okay, so there are no ads, no in-app purchases and they aren't taking information out of our messages, so how do they think they are going to make their billions of dollars back? It turns out, that they aren't giving us the full picture when it comes to encryption.

Romain Aubert, a blogger on freecodecamp.org in his article "Why I told my friends to stop using WhatsApp and Telegram" points out that while WhatsApp encrypts the contents of the message, it does NOT encrypt the "metadata" (Edward Snowden, in a tweet on 2nd November 2015, said "Are your readers having trouble understanding the term 'metadata'? Replace it with 'activity records'. That's what they are"). And given that WhatsApp now share your 'information' with Facebook, you can see the problem. It's not your messages that they want - it's the metadata associated with your messages, that they mine and sell on to Facebook (and other third parties perhaps?). You might be thinking that this is no big deal. Here are some examples of metadata mining:

- They know you rang a phone sex service at 2:24 am and spoke for 18 minutes. *But they don't know what you talked about.*
- They know you called the suicide prevention hotline ... *But the topic of the call remains a secret.*
- They know you spoke with an HIV testing service, then your doctor, then your health insurance company in the same hour. *But they don't know what was discussed.*
- They know you called a gynaecologist, spoke for a half hour, and then called the local Planned Parenthood's number later that day. *But nobody knows what you spoke about.*

When WhatsApp give Facebook your metadata (and other personal data), Facebook use it to target advertising at you. This is how they get their money back.

And the problem is further compounded by that fact that the messages you send on WhatsApp are end-to-end encrypted, meaning that *during transmission* your message is safe. How about when your messages are on your device. It is possible (and most people would have this setup as default), to make backups of your messages to either the iCloud (Apple devices) or Google Drive (Android devices). The unencrypted form of the message is the one that is backed up. As James Frew points out, "If someone wanted access to your messages, they would only need the latest copy of your daily backup. It is also vulnerable as there is no ability to change your backup location, meaning that you are at the mercy of the cloud service to keep your data protected". And here's an interesting fact - iCloud, in 2014, was responsible for the largest celebrity data leak in history.

Safety Tip #1: If you're worried about 'big brother' and what he's doing with your metadata, stop using WhatsApp and switch to Signal.

Safety Tip #2: Read the WhatsApp guidelines on staying safe. In particular, look at the paragraphs on seeing content; sharing content; reporting issues to WhatsApp; spam; blocking and banning people; hoaxes; suicide prevention, child abuse.

Facebook

Safety Tip #1: 'Friend Requests' are nothing more that Stranger Requests unless you can verify that you know the personal in real life. Never 'friend' a stranger. You should never accept a friend request from a person you do not know in real life. And it's not safe to accept a 'friend' request from someone who claims to be a friend of a friend. Always verify the identity of the person behind the 'friend' request *before* accepting it.

Safety Tip #2: Only post things that you are happy for the general public to see. There is every chance that the information you post will spread way beyond your original submission. The danger for children is their need for instant gratification. Take a selfie, post the selfie, look for 'views' and 'likes'. Selfies can contain two types of dangerous information: firstly the 'metadata' (hidden information in every image) can contain rich information about the image - gps coordinates; make and model of the camera or phone; in some cases, the serial number of the camera or phone etc. Secondly, the selfie can contain information in the image itself. For example, if your child takes a selfie in the school uniform, do they have a crest on the uniform? It's fairly easy to identify a school simply from a reverse image lookup on Google Images.

Safety Tip #3: Manage privacy. It has been estimated that 60% of Social Media users are unaware of the privacy settings in the various accounts. When we talk about children, this climbs to close to 90%. I believe as parents we need to be the privacy watchdogs for our children. Facebook is pretty good at providing assistance for setting privacy, but it is also infamous for changing privacy settings continually, and for NOT having a setting privacy by default to fully safe. Logically, Facebook (and the other Social Media systems) don't want us to be private. In fact, if 100% of Facebook users set their accounts to be 100% private, I wonder if Facebook would even survive! Here are three absolute musts for all parents (and users of Facebook in general):

1. Read the Facebook data policy. It's not as onerous as you

might expect. Give it as much time as you can - 10 minutes is about my limit. It'll open your eyes!

2. After you've killed a few brain cells reading the Facebook data policy, move on to the Facebook privacy help page. This is quite good - giving practical advice on preventing 'data leakage' (that you might have seen in the Data Policy you read earlier).

3. Okay, now that you understand the issues it's time to configure the Privacy Settings themselves. Remember, in Facebook there might be a couple of different 'settings' areas. If you have a Facebook page, as well as a Facebook account, you will need to address both settings (Facebook account settings; Facebook page settings).

Safety Tip #4: Beware of friend requests from 'real' friends. This is where you get a friend request from someone you DO know in real life. Here's the problem, it's easy to set up fake accounts. How do you know if the friend request really does come from a real friend? Note, you *cannot* get a second friend request from the same friend. If you are already friends with a person, and suddenly you receive a second friend request, something is up! Secondly, if you get a friend request from a person you actually know, but haven't to date hooked up with on Facebook, before accepting the friend request, verify that the account is actually genuine.

Safety Tip #5: If you ask kids what they think the biggest danger on the Internet is, they will almost always say "hacking". There is a lot of urban myth surrounding the word "hacker". Accounts are often 'hacked' but not by those super-human, evil genius 12-years old sitting the mummy's basement performing wizardry on their laptops. Most accounts get 'hacked' because the account holder has been either careless with account details, and/or has used *really* weak credentials. And most 'hacking' of Social Media accounts is carried out by individuals who personally know the victim.

So, as parents, you should be quizzing your kids about their credentials. I have included a chapter on Password safety later in the book (Chapter 8), but this tip is all about something called the "Friend in Distress" scheme. These occur where someone has 'hacked' an account (or otherwise gained access to someone's account), and then sends out messages to the list of friends in the account, claiming that they are in distress and need financial aid. NEVER respond unthinkingly to Friend in Distress requests. If you receive such a request, verify the source - pick up the phone and call the individual concerned.

Audience Suggestion #2: In one of the parents' seminars, a mother volunteered this suggestion: "In my house I have a rule. Every two weeks I inspect my child's Social Media accounts, and go through all friends and followers with her. If she is unable to accurately identify the real-life person behind each of her online friends and followers, she has to delete the individual from her lists"

Audience Suggestion #3: This is very sensible from a father in the audience. Privacy settings, Terms & Conditions and App Permissions are continuously changing. How can we as parents keep abreast of things? Well, this dad came up with a very simple trick.
1. Find out what apps your kids are using.
2. Install the app on your phone (you do not even have to sign up to the service). Simply having the app on the phone is sufficient.
3. Keep an eye on your phone, and when the apps ask to be updated - there's your signal to talk to your kids about the new privacy settings in the app.

There are many more social media platforms that I could go into here, but in the interests of brevity, I'm going to close this chapter with three last systems that you need to be aware of. I've selected the first two because they are extremely popular amongst the young people I talk to. However, my gut tells me that they will not have the same staying power as the systems above. The third one - Omegle - speaks for itself.

Musical.ly / Live.ly

What is it? From the musical.ly website: "musical.ly is a social media platform for creating and sharing short videos. Every day, millions of people around the world use musical.ly as an outlet for creative expression and communication with friends. musical.ly is a platform that connects individuals to a vibrant and highly-engaged community of content creators."

From the musical.ly Terms of Service agreement, "Eligibility. THE SERVICE IS NOT FOR PERSONS UNDER THE AGE OF 13 OR FOR ANY USERS PREVIOUSLY SUSPENDED OR REMOVED FROM THE SERVICE BY MUSICAL.LY. IF YOU ARE UNDER 13 YEARS OF AGE, YOU MUST NOT USE OR ACCESS THE SERVICE AT ANY TIME OR IN ANY MANNER. Furthermore, by using the Service, you affirm that either you are at least 18 years of age or have been authorized to use the service by your parent or guardian who is at least 18 years of age"

Forget the blurb, musical.ly is a free social media music app where users can watch user-generated videos, and create and publish video themselves. The videos are going to be either 'lip-syncing' or dancing to music available on the app. It has over 80 million users. You can choose your own music, or mix someone else video and create your own short music or audio video using filters and video styles. It is a fun app! Its companion app is called Live.ly which allows users to live-stream their videos to their audience.

According to the musical.ly parents' guide, "musical.ly's terms prohibits use of the app by anyone under the age of 13. Please do not allow your child under the age of 13 to use our apps.". This is interesting, because in my experience musical.ly is used almost exclusively by 8, 9 and 10-year-olds. 11-year-olds are already starting think it is 'not cool' to be on musical.ly and once you talk to secondary school students (who are the supposed target market for musical.ly), not a single one will admit to using it - it is simply 'too childish' for teens to be using.

Interestingly, the majority of primary-school children who are on musical.ly, have uploaded tens if not hundreds of videos of themselves. I met one 8-year girl who proudly boasted that she had 2500 musical.ly videos all publicly available. In fact, in one primary school I was in recently, the ENTIRE school was using musical.ly.

Here are the dangers you need to think about when allowing your child to use Musical.ly:

- There is nothing to stop users uploading inappropriate content. For example, pornography, graphic content, suicide notes, self-harm instructions etc.
- Musical.ly provides a facility for searching for other users based on geographical location.
- User generated videos can be viewed and shared via other social media and messaging apps.
- Bullying in comments is very common. Anyone posting videos of themselves and then allowing strangers to comment, needs to be prepared for abuse!
- Users can publicise their messenger usernames or social media profiles on their Musical.ly profile
- Live.ly live streaming is not private even if you have the privacy settings set up.
- It is easy to set up fake accounts. These can be used for bullying, grooming or other illegal activities.
- Inside the app there is no easy way to report accounts as being fake or underage.
- It's easy to create fake accounts and hide these from parents.

Safety Tip #1: Make sure you engage with your children when they talk about Musical.ly

Safety Tip #2: Remember, if your child is not yet thirteen, then it is against the rules for them to use musical.ly. If they are using musical.ly, then you as the parent need to take responsibility for this and everything that occurs in the App.

Safety Tip #3: Read the musical.ly Community Guidelines

Safety Tip #4: NEVER allow your child to use Live.ly unsupervised.

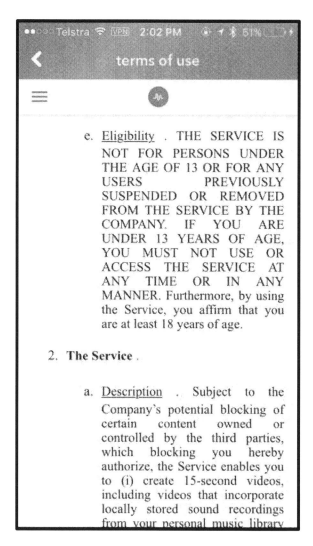

Yellow

 You could be forgiven for not having heard of Yellow (yellw.co). It has been dubbed "Tinder for Kids", it is being used by teenagers (from 13 years old and up) and it is not something that youngsters talk about to adults. So, you might well never have heard of it.

According to the Yellow Terms of Service, "Yellow allows you to make new chat friends". It's lower age limit is 13 and if the user is under the age of 18, they must have parental consent to use it.

It works like this: the teen signs up by simply typing their name, birthday, and gender. Yellow will then ask for a verification phone number, and once the account is verified, they'll be connected with other people within a 100km radius. The problem is there is no age verification, there is no verification of any of the facts! Anyone can set up an account using a fake name, image and claim to be any age. It is estimated that in excess of 30% of the accounts on Yellow are actually adults, posing as teens.

Safety Tip #1: You need to be aware of the things your children are doing on the Internet. I've said it before - you cannot simply abandon your children on the Internet. If you do, you are losing control and your children *will* almost certainly get into trouble.

Safety Tip #2: Understand the rules. If your child is under 13, they are not permitted to use Yellow. If your child is 13 to 17, then you as the legal guardian, have to give permission for them to have an account. This doesn't mean that someone is going to come knocking on your door check that you gave permission, but rather this puts the responsibility on your shoulders for your child's safety.

Safety Tip #3: Read the Yellow Community Guidelines

Omegle

 Omegle's tag line is "Talk to strangers". Anonymity is where it is at with Omegle. On their home page (omegle.com) you are given a few simple options:

- chat via text messages to complete, unidentified strangers.
- College student chat - you need a verified student email address for this.
- Video streaming. This is the most prominent thing on the page and has only one link - the "adult" link.

Chatting to strangers is simply weird and I don't believe is used that much. Most people gravitate to the adult video chat section. So, click on the link and the following happens:

1. A large pop-up appears with a warning: "You are about to go to a site with sexual material. IF YOU ARE UNDER 18, sexual material is illegal for you to view or possess, or you do not want to see that kind of material, PRESS CANCEL. By pressing OK, you affirm that you are at least 18 years old.". Click on the OKAY button.

2. You are then taken to a new site called My Free Cams. There is a pop-up covering the main screen asking you to set up your account. At the top of this popup, there is a 'minimise' button.

3. You then click on the minimise button, it seems that you can access any of the live webcams without any sort of age verification. In fact, you are accessing the site as a 'guest' which means that the video producer (or 'model') can mute your conversation.

These so called 'models' - the people that are producing these live streams, are making money doing this. The audience buys tokens through the site for real money. They then 'tip' the performer with tokens for doing various things. The performer then gets the money that the tokens represent - less a percentage to the site. Nothing is taboo - the audience can offer tokens for any activity imaginable.

Omegle says (at the bottom of their home page) "Omegle video chat is moderated. However, moderation is not perfect. You may still encounter people who misbehave. They are solely responsible for their own behaviour"!

Audience members will make off-line recordings of the videos, and there is nothing stopping them from distributing these videos to their own circle of friends and acquaintances.

And lastly, given the ease with which all of this is done, is it any surprise that children and teens are now frequenting Omegle - both as consumers of amateur pornography, and as *producers*. This is the truly shocking secret of child pornography: a growing proportion of it is produced by the victims themselves. According to the IWF (Internet Watch Foundation - a UK-based organisation that works with the authorities to try to remove online child pornography), as much as one third of all material they see is now self-generated - in other words the children themselves are making it.

Safety Tip #1: Do NOT allow anyone under the age of 18 to use Omegle!

Safety Tip #2: Take a look at the Omegle Privacy Policy. Probably the most inadequate policy possible. Last updated in June 2014. In terms of safety they put ALL responsibility on the parents of the children.

4 THE DANGERS OF APPS

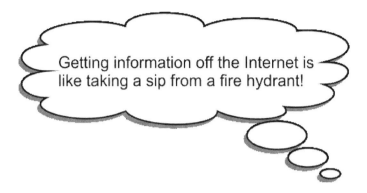

The number of mobile apps has grown at a phenomenal. Since its opening in the Summer of 2008, Apple's iTunes App Store has grown to well over 2.2 million - resulting in billions of app downloads, while Android users are able to choose from more than 2.8 million Apps!

Although the growth of apps is slowing, there are still on average an additional 600 new iOS apps appearing per day on the Apple Store! With are over 2.8 million apps on the Google Play Store, the latest figures show that this is increasing by 2500 apps per day or 100 new apps every hour!

It has become increasingly more difficult to protect our children from the available technology. Apps are now accepted as part of our daily life. For every good, useful, helpful app on the market there are as many dangerous, harmful apps readily available to our children.

Make sure the App is age appropriate

Apps are designed to suit different age groups. Some apps on the market have a recommended age as young as 6 months! There are thousands of apps available to children in the 2 to 4-year-old category. Generally, the recommended age range for each individual app comes from the developer. No-one knows your child better than you so therefore that makes you the best judge of whether a particular app is appropriate for your child.

Safety Considerations

Paedophiles, predators and Cyber Bullies are every bit as prominent in the app community as they are in online chat rooms and social networks. As a parent, you should be aware that not all app developers are trustworthy! Most of the apps our children download, do not require contact with other people, however they can be a very simple means of obtaining very personal information, capturing images of our children while playing games, simply by accessing files on the device.

Safety Tip #1: The first thing you need to do before downloading any app is to check exactly what the app will need to access – this is the 'permissions'. This can be done by either clicking on the 'Install' button or the 'Read More' link. Once you click on the 'Install' button and before the App actually downloads on to your phone, you are presented with a pop up window which lists what the app will actually access if you proceed to download it.

<u>This is equivalent to handing your unlocked phone over to a complete stranger!</u>

Some of the more dangerous apps require access to all the information available on your phone. At this point you need to stop and think carefully before agreeing to download the app.

What type of data do some apps want to access?

Do you really want some faceless corporation to:

40

- have access to all the images stored on your phone?
- have access to your camera – some apps have been known to take photos using your camera without your knowledge (possible only if you agree to install the app)?
- have access to your entire contact list (mobile numbers and email addresses of family & friends)?
- have access to the location of the phone? Some apps can automatically turn on the GPS locator on the phone. Think of the consequences of this in particular if it is your child's phone?
- read all of your emails?
- have access to the metadata associated with all of the images taken on your phone (e.g. the date the image was taken or the location)?
- have access to your entire browser history?
- have access to all the files which store data in the memory of your device?
- have access to all of your social media platforms?
- have access to all of your messages (text messages, WhatsApp, SnapChat, Messenger, etc)?

To be perfectly clear, we often cannot know the extent of the things we agree to when we download apps as the descriptions can be intentionally very vague. Remember this, we may well be installing *malicious* software - which might, for instance, sit on our phone and mine our passwords as we input them!

We cannot prevent our children from downloading apps but you can teach your child to be savvy and check the permissions that are required. Get them to consider whether they really need that particular app (particularly once they have reviewed apps permissions).

How do free apps make their money?

Think of all the time and money that has been invested into developing a particular app. If it is a free app and does not contain any advertisements then how do the developers make their money?

The answer is simple – they mine the information from your phone and sell it on to third parties. Businesses exist primarily to make money so they will often sell your information to the highest bidder. Although this is a perfectly legitimate business model, and in fact the companies are able to do it because we give them permission to do it, the problem is that there is little to stop criminals from using the same process.

A Popular App is not always a Safe App!

In 2014/15 one of the most popular games on the Android Play store was a simple game called 'Crossy Roads' (at the time of writing, primary school kids are still playing it). The aim of the game was very simple, to get your little game character safely across a busy road. The task got progressively harder as the game progressed. This game currently has in excess of 50 million downloads!

When the game first appeared on the scene, it quickly became obvious that it was one of the most widely played and well-known games downloaded by Primary School children. Our review of the game at the time showed that it required access to all of the files on the device when installed. This was particularly worrying as there were reports at the time of the app actually taking images of the person playing the game, using the front facing camera (see illustration above). Here is a list of the permissions required by Crossy Roads:

Location
- precise location (GPS and network-based)
- approximate location (network-based)

Photos/Media/Files
- modify or delete the contents of your USB storage
- read the contents of your USB storage

Wi-Fi connection information
- view Wi-Fi connections

Device ID & call information
- read phone status and identity

Other
- full network access
- view network connections

To put this in context, it is on a par with allowing a photographer, who is a complete stranger to you and your family, to enter your child's bedroom and take photos of your child as they lie in bed, playing the game.

Children can also often be found playing their 'innocent games' on devices while lying in the bath, on the beach and even from time to time while sitting on the toilet! While we have no proof that any game actually takes photos of your child, you, as a parent should always err on the side of caution and check the permissions. Ask yourself 'Why does a simple game need access to my GPS location, my camera, my contact list or my message files'?

Harmful apps parents should be aware of:

There are too many apps to list individually but it is worth putting the time and effort into checking the apps that your children are currently using.

Read the reviews, check the age rating and search for the app on the Internet to find out what other parents are saying about it.

You should also teach your child to ask permission before downloading a new App. This will allow you time to research it in full before agreeing or disagreeing with the download.

Just some examples of apps that you should be wary of are:

Tinder	Sim Simi	Yik Yak
Ask.fm	Vine	Kik Messenger
Yellow	Shots of Me	Voxer
Monkey	Tumblr	Poke Rated as 4+
Down	Whisper	Burn Note
Omegle	After School	Periscope
Musical.ly		

(Yellow is an app designed to look similar to Snapchat. It has been described as "Tinder for kids")

Hiding things from parents?

There are a number of different ways that children (in particular teens) be secretive and keep their information hidden from their parents.

If they decide that they want to hide images, there are a number of apps out there that will come to their rescue. These apps are often designed to look like everyday simple apps but they contain a secret hidden vault. For example, there are many designed to look and function as a normal calculator would. It is only when you input a secret PIN number that the vault opens allowing the user to store nude selfies, and other sexting material.

Try it for yourself - search on the Google Play Store for 'Calculator Photo Vault' and you will be amazed at the number of options available!

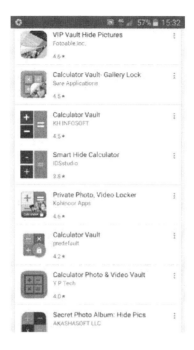

Of the first 12 options, available on the Play Store at the time of writing there were at least two of the apps that have been downloaded over 10 million times, (Gallery Vault and Keep Safe).

How do teens hide apps from parents?

Not only are images hidden from parents, but so are a whole range of inappropriate apps. Again, there are a range of vault-type apps that will store anything you need (e.g. messages from different messaging platforms, videos, inappropriate apps).

Vault-Hide, Vaulty, Master Lock Vault, App Lock, Security Master, Perfect App Lock, App Lock Fingerprint and Poof are all examples of vault type apps that teens are using to hide other apps.

Safety Tip #2: Check the user reviews of all apps – before installing them.

Safety Tip #3: All apps ask you for permission to access various features of your device. Always read the permissions list BEFORE installing an app.

Safety Tip #4: Keep your eyes and ears open for information on new apps trending now.

Safety Tip #5: Talk to your children and make them aware of the dangers of harmful apps.

5 PERSISTENCE OF INFORMATION: YOUR REPUTATION AT RISK

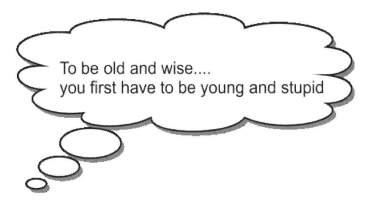

To be old and wise....
you first have to be young and stupid

A couple of years ago, Kevin[1], a recent 'high-flying' graduate from the University of Limerick, applied for and was invited to an initial interview for a senior managerial role in a local motor car dealership. Kevin is a supremely confident individual having always excelled at anything he put his hand to - including his degree, at which he got the best results of his year group.

In the invitation that he received from the company, there was some small print which informed all candidates that the Company reserved the right to look at candidates Social Media presence, as part of the interview process. This did not bother Kevin, because he didn't use Social Media.

He attended the first interview for the job along with around 20 other candidates. As expected, he was invited back for a second interview - this time with 5 other candidates. After this second interview, the number was whittled down to two candidates for a third and final interview, this one with the CEO of the organisation. Kevin was, unsurprisingly, one of the two finalists.

---

[1] Name changed to protect identity

He turned up to the final interview, fully expecting to be offered the position. To his surprise, before he was able to contribute to the interview, the CEO - very politely - informed Kevin that he would not be getting the job. Kevin was flabbergasted. This was probably the first time in his life that he had experienced failure. Kevin asked the CEO if he could know the reasons. The CEO informed Kevin that it was as a result of his Social Media presence. Kevin, now a little annoyed, told the CEO that that wasn't possible - he didn't use Social Media. The CEO (again very politely) told Kevin that it wasn't *his* Social Media accounts - but those of his friends. Kevin had featured in hundreds of compromising situations on *other people's* Social Media pages!

It is becoming more and more common for HR departments of large organisations to access individuals' Social Media profiles prior to offers of employment. The problem is that once you've posted something to your profile, it is impossible to control its distribution. Once you've posted something to the Internet, you need to understand that you cannot get it back.

Another real-life story: A father told me this story during one of my parents talks. He, the father, is a freelance journalist. He writes for a living and often has to sell his writing to publications etc. When he was a 'hot-headed' young student close on 20 years ago, he proudly wrote an article and published it to an online Bulletin Board. The article was full of youthful passion and black & white fundamentalism, and has come back to haunt him on many occasions - particularly if he is bidding for work. Whenever anyone wants to look at his work, his article from his student days, tops the search engine lists. There is nothing he can do about it. He has to justify his extreme views every single time anyone finds that article.

What makes information that you post to the Internet so permanent? There are a few factors at play here:

1. Generally, when you post something to the Internet, it is transported to its final destination, never directly, but almost always via a circuitous route - hitting lots of different Internet servers before getting to its intended destination. Each of the transit servers can and generally will, retain a copy of the information.
2. Anyone, once they see an article, picture, message etc. can make their own copies of it - either for their own use or simply to distribute to their own circle of friends and acquaintances.
3. Most Social Media companies, through their Terms of Service and other policy documents, reserve the right to use the information that is being posted to and on their systems. For example, Instagram states in its Terms of Use document "Instagram does not claim ownership of any content that you post on or through the Service. Instead, *you hereby grant to Instagram a non-exclusive, fully paid and royalty-free, transferable, sub-licensable, worldwide license to use the Content that you post on or through the Service*".

Safety Tip #1: Understand a fundamental rule of the Internet, namely that once you post something (send, post, publish etc.), YOU LOSE CONTROL OVER HOW IT IS ULTIMATELY USED.

Safety Tip #2: As a parent, you need to hammer this point home to you children, from the day they start participating on Social Media sites. Teenagers, who are publishing every minute of their lives to the World, need to realise that images etc posted when they are very young and innocent, will still be there when they are looking for University places, Internships and Jobs - and that their online timeline might well be scrutinised by prospective employers etc.

Safety Tip #3: Take a look at the video entitled "Amazing mind reader reveals his gift" on YouTube (the easiest way to find this video is to search for "Dave the mind reader").

6 YOUR CHILD AND THE LAW

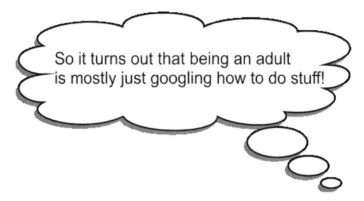

So it turns out that being an adult is mostly just googling how to do stuff!

I am not a legal expert. However, having spoken to many legal professionals and law enforcement authorities I believe I have an understanding of the legal issues that might benefit readers. Remember though, <u>if you are ever in a position where you need legal counsel - you must seek professional legal advice from qualified professionals.</u>

Living and working in the Republic of Ireland, my most up-to-date information is based on the Irish legal system, which in turn is influenced by European law. Many of the laws in Ireland are mirrored to a large extent throughout the countries of Europe. And looking wider afield, most 'first-world' countries have similar legal frameworks.

It doesn't matter which jurisdiction you reside in, you need to understand a few fundamentals:
1. My right to privacy trumps everything. If I find that you have posted an image onto your Instagram account (for arguments sake), that features me - I have a right to request that you take it down. This extends to tagging in photos and geotagging of images. In 2016 there was a case in Austria, where a 16-year old girl found that her mother had posted pictures of her on the mother's Facebook account, from when the she was a baby. The 16-year took offense at this and asked her mum to take the pictures down. The mother refused, so the daughter,

under Austrian law, was able to sue her mother and she won. The mother was forced by the courts to take the pictures down.

2. Cyber bullying is against the law in many countries, although it is probably not called cyberbullying. For example, in Ireland, it falls under a much wider umbrella of libel; defamation of character, slander etc. In the USA, every state has its own take on Cyberbullying.

3. "child pornography" is defined as a sexually explicit image of a person under the age of consent (which varies from country to country) and the possession of such images, is illegal. The law does not necessarily make exceptions if the person in the image is yourself! In other words, if your child has taken a 'naked selfie' (or 'nude' as kids call them), they are technically in possession of child pornography and can be prosecuted.

4. If a child has taken a 'nude' they are now in possession of child pornography. If they've pressed 'Send' on their phones and sent that 'nude' to a friend - they have broken a second law - they are now guilty of *distribution* of child pornography - possibly an even graver offense.

5. If you as the parent have done what a lot of parents do and 'tied' their children's accounts to their own accounts - so that they can monitor what their children are doing, and if your child has taken a 'nude', then *you* are now in possession of child pornography, and you won't not even be aware of it.

6. Things have a habit of hanging around on the Internet. Nothing is ever really deleted, and images that your children take as kids, are still going to be on devices and accounts long after they are grown up. A child would probably not be severely punished for having a couple of naked selfies on their phones. However, if they are adults and still have naked images from when they were kids, that might be a different issue altogether.

Unfortunately, the scope of this book does not permit us to look at the laws in each jurisdiction. In the reference chapter at the end of the book, you'll find links to a lot of websites for different jurisdictions. Please do your own research for your particular location. Here is a summary of current legislation in Ireland:

Current[2] Legislation in Ireland

The current legislation which governs bullying in Ireland is as follows:

Section 2 of the Non-Fatal Offences Against the Person Act 1997 sets out the offence of assault as follows:

- A person shall be guilty of the offence of assault who, without lawful excuse, intentionally or recklessly causes another to believe on reasonable grounds that he or she is likely immediately to be subjected to any such force or impact, without the consent of the other.

Section 5 of the Non-Fatal Offences Against the Person Act 1997 sets out the offence of assault as follows:

- A person who, without lawful excuse, makes to another a threat, by any means intending the other to believe it will be carried out, to kill or cause serious harm to that other or a third person shall be guilty of an offence.

Section 10 of the Non Fatal Offences Against the Person Act 1997 sets out the offence of harassment as follows:

- Without lawful authority or reasonable excuse, by any means including by use of the telephone, harasses another by persistently following, watching, pestering, besetting or communicating with him or her, shall be guilty of an offence."

If a student is physically beaten or has been put in a reasonable belief of immediate force, the perpetrator will be guilty of assault under section 2 of the 1997 Act.

When a student has threatened to kill or cause serious harm to another and expects that student to believe the threat, this may constitute an offence under section 5 of the 1997 Act.

---

[2] as of July 2017

If a student is harassed by another student it may constitute an offence under section 10 of the 1997 Act.

 The Education Act 1998 states that the responsibility that children's needs are met rests with the school's board of management. Schools in Ireland do not have a set of laws to follow in cases of bullying. Since the Education (Welfare) Act 2000 all schools in Ireland are under a legal duty to have a written code of behavior. The code of behavior states, "the standards of behavior that shall be observed by each student attending the school; the measures that may be taken when a student fails or refuses to observe those standards; procedures and the grounds for removing a suspension imposed in relation to a student". The 2000 Act does not make any reference to the term 'Bullying'.

The main Irish law dealing with Data Protection is the Data Protection (Amendment) Act 2003 and covers all matters of data protection on all types of platforms, whether they are telephone, computer, email, etc. The Acts allow for remedies where a breach or release of information has occurred.

- Another legal remedy available to deal with cyberbullying is the implementation of **Usage Policy**. This would involve contacting the relevant medium or platform on which the cyberbullying is taking place and requesting that all information be removed and that the usage policy is enforced against the perpetrator.
- **Defamation**: A "defamatory statement" means a statement that tends to injure a person's reputation in the eyes of reasonable members of society, statements made online, whether they appear in social media sites, twitter, email etc., are not immune to the laws on defamation. If a defamatory statement is made then civil redress can be claimed through the courts.
- **Injunction**: This is a court order that can either prohibit the publication of certain information or force its removal.

Ireland has ratified agreements for the promotion and protection of Children's rights. The United Nations Convention on the Rights of the Child 1989 (CRC) is the most significant. The main Article which gives children the right to be educated without violence is Article 19 which states, "parties shall take all appropriate legislative, administrative, social and educational measures to protect the child from all forms of physical or mental violence, injury or abuse, neglect or negligent treatment, maltreatment or exploitation, including sexual abuse, while in the care of parent(s), legal guardian(s) or any other person who has the care of the child"

Culpability:
- In civil cases, parents may be held liable or accountable for the actions and conduct of their children in certain circumstances. These circumstances would depend on the facts of each individual case.
- Schools and similar institutions have an operating duty of care to those in their care. Culpability for cyberbullying can attach to the school or institution in certain limited circumstances. Liability can arise due to the non-implementation of school policies which would allow unmonitored access to the internet through computers or smartphones (and soon smartwatches).

2 bills currently passing through the Seanad are as follows:

1. HARMFUL AND MALICIOUS ELECTRONIC COMMUNICATIONS ACT 2015 (introduced by Senator Lorraine Higgins - recently passed the Second Stage in the Seanad)
- Summary: An Act to protect against and mitigate harm caused to individuals by all or any digital communications and to provide such individuals with a means of redress for any such offending behaviours directed at them.

- A person guilty of an offence under this section shall be liable on summary conviction to a fine not exceeding €5,000 or imprisonment for a term not exceeding 12 months or to both.
- The court can order that the person remove or delete specific electronic communication(s);(b) that the person shares an apology or correction as the court deems appropriate in the circumstances;(c) that the person shall not, for such period as the court may specify, communicate by any means with the other person or that the person shall not approach within such distance as the court shall specify of the place of residence or employment of the other person.

2. PUBLIC ELECTRONIC COMMUNICATIONS NETWORKS (Improper Use) ACT, 2015 (introduced by Minister Pat Rabbitte)

Summary: An Act to make it an offence for a person to send, or cause to be sent, by means of a public electronic communications network a message or other matter that is grossly offensive or menacing in character.

Safety Tip #1:   Speak with your children about the legal implications of the Social Media usage.

Safety Tip #2: Monitor your children's Internet usage. Talk to them regularly about what apps they are using and how they are using them.

What is the age of digital consent?

The EU General Data Protection Regulation will come into effect in May 2018 and this allows for member states to set their own age of digital consent. The new EU Regulations suggest an age range of between 13 to 16 and here in Ireland we have opted for the lower age. In July 2017, the Irish Government decided to set the "Age of Digital Consent" at 13.

This means that data controllers (i.e. those responsible for storing personal data) are not permitted to store any data gathered from any child below the age of 13. Parental consent is required up to the age of 13 and thereafter, consent can be given by the individual themselves during the registration process, when setting up an account or when downloading an app.

The main problem is that most of the well-known social media platforms already have their own minimum age requirements already in place. These do not necessarily stop a child under the recommended age of inputting a false date of birth if they really want to sign up for a particular service without their parents' knowledge! There is no requirement, under current legislation, to verify a person's date of birth, so in effect anyone can, sign up for anything. How many  websites have you visited or games have you played where a large warning comes up on screen, alerting you to the fact that the game is not suitable for anyone under the age of 18. Do you honestly believe that this will stop your child from going ahead and playing the game, or watching films and programmes above their age group? Not for one second!

If a child under the age of 13 goes to the cinema and tries to get in to an over 18's movie, it is almost guaranteed that they will be turned away by the ticket seller or the usher. These are effective controls and work well in the majority of situations. Relying on a child to input their correct date of birth is not a strong enough or an effective control. It is just another example of how the legislation is trailing behind technology. Technology is moving at such a fast pace that it seems like a huge task for Governments to keep track of developments and try to keep our most vulnerable members of society, our children, safe.
From my own perspective, it actually seems quite simple really!

Governments must make the large corporations take on the responsibility of protecting our children. Don't get me wrong, setting the "Age of Digital Consent" at 13 is a welcome step but, will it actually lead to a change in behaviour?

It is frightening to see just how quickly a tech savvy child can access the most inappropriate content or the worst pornography imaginable.

As parents, we know only too well that our children will try every way possible to bend the rules or find a way to get around a particular control. There is nothing really that prevents a 10-year-old from accessing a hardcore pornographic site at the moment. That needs to change as unfettered access to such content will influence our children's generation in a way that will be difficult to reverse.

Governments need to do more, that is for certain. In the short- to medium-term, the most effective controls we have as parents are the controls we put in place for our children – good old-fashioned parenting techniques!

7 CYBER BULLYING AND THE ROLE OF THE SCHOOL

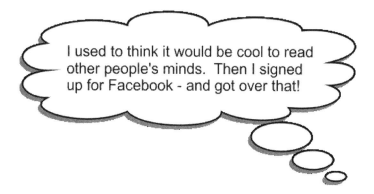

What is Bullying and how is it different to Cyber bullying?

"Bullying is when someone repeatedly threatens, harasses, mistreats, or makes fun of another person (on purpose)". Cyber Bullying is just another form of bullying where the victim is usually targeted on one (or a combination) of the Social Media platforms, via text messages, emails or websites.

Cyber Bullying has grown over the last 10 years in direct proportion to the growth in our use of social media and the Internet.

Research:

In Ireland, a recent study has shown that up to 14% of students aged 12-16 have been cyber bullied, while 9% reported that they have bullied others in this way.
Incidence rates for cyber-bullying tend to be slightly higher amongst girls than boys.

The **'Growing Up in Ireland'** study highlights how over 24% of 9 to 17-year olds have reported been bullied, while research by the Anti-Bullying Centre Trinity College has highlighted how one in four girls and one in six boys in Ireland have come in contact with cyber-bullying either as a victim, bully or both.

According to recent EU Kids Online research, 99% of young people aged 9 to 16 in Ireland, use the Internet. Over half of these have set up their own profile on a social networking site. Ofcom in the UK report that most kids are spending more than twice as much time on the web as their parents think they are – an average of 43.5 hours per month as opposed to the 18.8 hours that parents estimate. Internet use is thoroughly embedded in the everyday lives of young people and is often without any form of supervision from parents. Many young people are accessing the internet from their bedrooms rather than other rooms in the house.

According to a recent report in the Irish Times "Almost two thirds of Irish teenagers described cyber bullying as being worse than face-to-face bullying while just over half said it was a bigger problem than drug abuse for young people".

A few more interesting facts:

- Suicide has increased in proportion to the increase in use of Social Media
- Young people on Social Media are twice as likely to commit suicide than those that are not on Social Media.

What is the role of the School?

The school plays a very important role in dealing with Cyber Bullying and matters relating to keeping your child safe while on the Internet (at School). The responsibility of putting an effective anti-cyber bullying policy in place lies with the Principal. The policy is used to put preventative measures in place, determine how situations are dealt with, offer supports to those involved, put a strategy in place to avoid future issues arising and monitoring current issues.

However, parents, most if not all cyber bullying, happens *outside of the school environment*, and teachers and other educators cannot be expected to 'fix' problems that occur outside of school!

What are the key elements in the prevention of Bullying?

Schools who have reported success in the battle against Bullying are usually found to have a very pro-active Principal who allocates time and support to the implementation of the school anti-bullying policy.

This can often include fully supporting the staff to implement an intervention program.

Teachers are encouraged to intervene at an early stage in the escalation of bullying situations. School staff, who have participated in a prevention program generally feel more empowered to intervene in all types of potential bullying situations.

Through the training received, they will also have a better understanding of the situation, have greater empathy towards the victim and are better equipped to liaise with both the parents of the victim and the bully.

Many children do not report their bullying experience to the teacher so teachers must be aware at all times, (both during class time and in the yard) of situations that may escalate into bullying.

The level of supervision in areas of the school that have not been particularly well monitored in the past needs to be increased in order to prevent the escalation from horseplay to bullying. These include corridors, gym areas, the school yard, bicycle shelters, toilet areas, etc

What can the School do about Cyber Bullying?

The school has many tools to help minimise the extent of Cyber Bullying in the School. Some examples are set out below:

- Minimise the use of mobile phones during school hours.
- Have Firewalls in place to filter / prevent certain social media platforms.
- Use class time to encourage victims to speak out and not to bottle up an issue. A bully will often rely on the victim to remain silent and by speaking to their parent or a teacher, the bully will often lose the hold they have over their victim.
- Ensure that the school anti-bullying policy clearly sets out the consequences of bullying behaviour and stick to these, ensuring that they are enforced.
- Involve the relevant authorities at an early stage and assist them in whatever way necessary during their investigation.
- Keep those involved and affected by the Cyber-Bullying in the loop. Keep the lines of communication open always.

- Ensure there are adequate numbers of staff trained in how to spot early signs of bullying behaviour before the situation escalates. Ensure they are trained in how to deal with bullying situations and trained in how to monitor the after effects of bullying.

What does a typical School Anti Bullying Policy contain?

 School Policies can vary to a large degree and many schools would include Cyber Bullying as a sub section of their overall Bullying Policy. Below are some of the main points that a standard Policy should have:

- An Introduction which should set out the aims or the role of the school in relation to Bullying.
- A Policy should always include the definition of Bullying, (while a modern version should include a definition of Cyber Bullying).
- A list of the types of Bullying covered by the Policy (e.g. Physical, Verbal, Psychological, Cyber / Online)
- The signs of Bullying or its effects on a child.
- A set of procedures for dealing with Bullying. These should be clearly set out so that they can easily be followed by the parent if necessary.
- A section outlining how each Bullying situation should be monitored and reviewed (including the responsibilities of the Bully, their parents, the school staff and the BoM)
- A paragraph which looks at the bigger picture and the implementation of measures that deals with the prevention of Bullying on an ongoing basis.
- A set of criteria by which the success of the Policy can be gauged.

What you can do if you believe that your child is being bullied?

1. Sit with your child and listen to their story. Try not to get angry and listen with empathy.
2. Stay calm and do not interrupt or offer advice until you have all the details from the child. Do NOT ask leading questions.
3. If you are dealing with cyber-bullying, ask your child to show you some examples. Take screen shots of all of the evidence and keep a copy in case it is required at a later date.
4. Try to build up a picture of how frequently it occurs and who your child thinks may be behind it.
5. DO NOT, under any circumstances contact the person (or their family) directly yourself.
6. DO contact the school. Ask to speak directly to the person with responsibility for Bullying in the school, (as they are usually trained in how best to deal with bullying situations) and arrange a meeting.
7. Make the school aware of the situation if they are not already aware and from there contact the authorities.
8. Familiarize yourself with the School's Anti- Bullying Policy and ensure the appropriate steps are taken by the school.
9. Take a calm approach. Re-assure your child that the situation will be dealt with through the proper channels, (the child will feel a weight lifted from their shoulders having spoken to an adult about their problem).

A Summary of the Do's and Don'ts of Cyber Bullying

Safety Tip #1: Your Child should:
1. NEVER EVER respond to a bully

2. NEVER EVER 'like' / retweet / re-post or in any way be supportive of bullying behaviour.
3. Keep Evidence / Take Screen Shots
4. ALWAYS report bullying to:
   1. Parents
   2. HOTLINE.IE
   3. If necessary to the Gardaí (or police).

Safety Tip #2: Research the apps your kids are using. Know how to use the "block", "ban" and "report" features of the system.

Safety Tip #3: If bullying continues – delete the account and start afresh – never giving out details to anyone other than family and real friends.

Safety Tip #4: NEVER OVER REACT when your child talks to you about cyber bullying.

In conclusion, while home used to be the place a child seeks refuge from the outer world where traditional bullying takes place, cyber bullying is penetrative in its nature. It invades the brick-and-cement walls of home and into the very fragile mind of the child.

8 SCAMS, MALWARE AND PASSWORD SECURITY

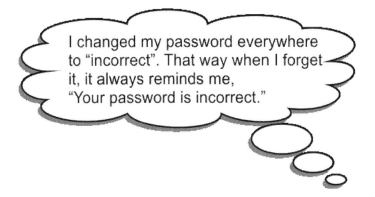

I changed my password everywhere to "incorrect". That way when I forget it, it always reminds me, "Your password is incorrect."

A school principal told me this story about his sister. She received an email from PayPal asking her to verify her account details. A couple of days later

she had lost €2500 from her PayPal account. You've probably heard similar stories. The email the woman had received obviously did not originate from PayPal and is just one of billions of similar scam emails in circulation.

One of the Netflix Black Mirror series episodes features Kenny a young man who has predilections towards paedophilia. He lends his

laptop to his sister. When he gets it back, he uses it to view illegal images on-line. What he doesn't realise is that his sister inadvertently clicked on a link on one of her websites, which infected Kenny's laptop with Spyware. While he is viewing the illegal images, unbeknownst to him, a shadowy organisation is now able to take control of his camera and take compromising pictures of him. They then use those compromising images to blackmail him.

While the Kenny story is fiction, the technology exists to carry out such attacks. Gangs of cybercriminals in South Korea and Japan are now using advanced Android apps that can steal private data and record conversations for sex extortion (sextortion) and blackmail.

You might have read about the "biggest cyberattack the world has ever seen". It happened over the weekend of the 12th, 13th and 14th of May 2017 and consisted of a virus called WannaCry that locks people out of their computer files until they pay a ransom in BitCoin cryptocurrency to

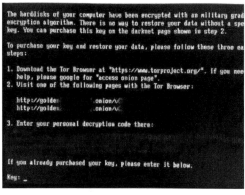

the hackers. Because of the nature of BitCoin, it is quite easy to get a view of how much money has been paid by victims. Keith Collins has set up a twitter 'bot' that provides a daily update on the amount of Bitcoin the attackers have received. You can follow it on Twitter using @actual_ransom. At the time of writing this chapter, the victims of the WannaCry attack have paid the attackers a total of 52.196

BitCoin. For someone not familiar with BitCoin and cryptocurrencies, that doesn't sound like much. It actually translates into US$135,000! To date the attackers have made no withdrawals of their ill-gotten gains.

The issue that we face as users of the Internet, is the bewildering number of different types of attacks that we might fall victim of: Trojans, rootkits, spyware, adware, ransomware, viruses to name but a few. However, I have not been a victim of any sort of attack in the last 15 years because I religiously follow two very simple strategies. Firstly, I have the best Antivirus software that I can get. There are two categories of antivirus software - commercial, and free. The free ones easily match up to the commercial ones, so it is really your choice. You will need to do some research before settling on an antivirus solution. I have found that the

PCMag site provides excellent up-to-date information and I would recommend visiting the site: uk.pcmag.com. They provide a search box (top right of the screen), type in "antivirus" and you'll be presented with a long list of articles. When I did the search while writing this chapter, the first two articles listed were what I required: "The Best Antivirus Protection of 2017" and "The Best Free Antivirus Protection of 2017".

Obviously, if you are reading this book in a year other than 2017, then you'll be looking for more up-to-date articles.

The second strategy that has protected me over the years, and arguably, the most important strategy, is simply I have a healthy dose of good old-fashioned common sense and mistrust. I mistrust everything - every email I get, every website I visit, every App I have on my phone. I mistrust the lot. I don't care who made it, who sent it, where it supposedly originated from - I don't trust it. This means that I ALWAYS check

every link, every attachment, every clickable thing before clicking on anything or downloading anything, and because I have been this paranoid for so long, I have trained my brain to recognise, subconsciously, that something is not right. If I feel uneasy about a link - no matter how innocent or 'real' it looks, I will examine it forensically before clicking on it. I look for some obvious signs of mischief:

- No organisation will ever ask you to provide login credentials via email. In fact, if you think about it logically, the organisation that you have an account with doesn't need your credentials - they already have them!
- Email addresses that look familiar, but on closer inspection are

slightly off. For example, "info@paypall.com". The real PayPal domain name (the bit that appears after the "@" sign), is spelled with a single "L" - so it should have been "info@paypal.com".

- Domain names that are slightly off. For example, "www.amazon.com.com" (notice the two ".com"s?).
- Even if a link looks perfect (e.g. www.amazon.com) what you are seeing is simply the display text - the actual link behind the text can be fake. A famous example was indeed a fake email people received from Amazon in 2007. In the body of the message, it asked the reader to click on the www.amazon.com link. A lot of people were surprised when they did click on the link to discover that their computers were now infected with malicious software. The link they had actually clicked on was "citdsl.fix.netvision.net.il" (Please DO NOT visit this link!).
- Someone offers you money - or tells you that you've won something. There is nothing free in this world - do NOT get excited if it appears that you are the recipient of some lottery winnings or inheritance.
- If an email starts with "My Dear" - I immediately delete it. No-one that I know would ever refer to me in that way.
- If an email or website contains spelling and grammatical errors. Obviously, everyone is prone to making the odd typo now and again. It's the clear grammatical errors and numerous spelling mistakes and misuse of words that get my defences up.

Safety Tip #1: Install good antivirus software on your devices. Many devices are shipped with a trial version of an antivirus package. I would immediately uninstall this trial version (it's a marketing ploy after all), and install a package of your choosing. We recommend Kaspersky anti-virus (www.kaspersky.com).

And don't forget your mobile devices! The top 5 antivirus apps for iPhone are:
- Kaspersky

- Lookout (by Lookout Inc.)
- McAfee Mobile Security
- MobiShield (by TrustMobi)
- Norton Mobile Security

The top 5 antivirus apps for Android are:
- Kaspersky
- AVG Antivirus Security
- TrustGo Antivirus and Mobile Security

- Avast! Mobile Security and Antivirus
- BitDefender Mobile Security and Antivirus

Safety Tip #2: Never click on links in emails and on websites without first checking them out. If the link in an email says, for example, www.amazon.com, instead of clicking on the link - open your browser and type the link into the address bar. This will ensure you don't click on a 'spoof' link.

Safety Tip #3: Watch out for "you are in this video" links - these are irresistible - who wouldn't want to see themselves starring in a video? 99% of the time they are traps and the links are malicious.

Password Security

Clicking fake links and downloading fake attachments is only one method by which we can fall victim of scams and other attacks. When talking to children in primary schools, I talk to them about "dangerous people". They immediately assume I'm talking about "hackers". I have to tell them that although "hackers" and "hacking" are definitely a problem, most people are never going to be victims of it - most people are victims of their own carelessness. And I am frequently told, by kids, of real-world examples of where they've been

hacked. They are actually referring to where an unknown person has taken over their Social Media account - not really about hacking.

Many people have experienced a violation of their Social Media accounts - but it is almost never by 'hackers' - it is almost always by someone they know who has got their credentials. This happens in two ways, either the person has given their credentials out to so-called 'friends' or, their credentials are so weak that they are easily guessed by someone who has a little knowledge about the person.

Fraping . dictionary results

Frape noun, verb, fraped, frap·ing.

-noun
1. The unlawful act of Facebook identity theft after the victim forgets to log out.
2. Complete destruction of an account on the social networking site Facebook.

-verb
3. to change status, religion and/or sexual orientation of a Facebook user.

The biggest issue sounding login credentials, is not that those credentials are weak, but that individuals will use the same credentials for every online account that they have. Once a person gets hold of your password for say Facebook, the odds are that they now have your password for Instagram, Twitter etc.

In summary, the two issues with passwords are that firstly, they are weak to start off with and secondly, they are repeated across all of our accounts. We need to address both issues.

Instead of making a *password* you need to make a *password rule or formula*. This rule determines how you create your passwords. If the rule is based on the name of the thing you need the password for, every password you generate using your rule will be unique. And here's the best bit - all you have to do is memorise the rule - and you will never have to remember a password ever again! Here is an example rule that I provide to kids and students as part of my talk:

Example Password Rule
1. Start with the name of the thing you want a password for. Let's say, for this example, that you're going to set up a new Gmail account. So, start with "Gmail".

2. Choose a favourite phrase (This will always remain constant - across all passwords).
3. Intersperse the name (from point 1) as capitals between the letters of the phrase (point 2) as lowercase.
4. Add your favourite year to the end.
5. Add a dollar sign to the end of that.

That is my 5-step rule for creating passwords. I memorise the rule and then use it EVERY time I need to generate a password. And here's the neat thing about it - if I ever forget my password, I can work it out by applying the rule again. Let's see it in action:

For Gmail:
1. Take the name of the thing: "Gmail"
2. My chosen phrase is "whenimsixtyfour"
3. Intersperse the name between the letters of the phrase: "wGhMeAnIiLmsixtyfour"
4. Add my favourite year to the end: "wGhMeAnIiLmsixtyfour1962"
5. Add a dollar sign to the end of that: "wGhMeAnIiLmsixtyfour1962$"

And there you have it - a highly secure password, containing, upper and lower-case characters, numbers and symbols - and I never (I actually couldn't) have to memorise it - when I need to get back into my Gmail account, I can simply apply the rule again.

Here's my Facebook password using the same rule: "wFhAeCnEiBmOsOiKxtyfour1962$"

Here's my Twitter password using the same rule: "wThWeInTiTmEsRixtyfour1962$"

Here's my Instagram password using the same rule: "wIhNeSnTiAmGsRiAxMtyfour1962$"

Two-factor Authentication

Two Factor Authentication

Two-factor authentication (2FA), adds an extra step to your basic log-in procedure. Without 2FA, you enter in your username and password, and then you're done. The password is your single factor of authentication. The second factor makes your account more secure, in theory.

Depending on the system the second factor of authentication could be a pin number sent to a mobile phone (very common), or an App that generates a unique OTC (one-time code) that you have to enter in addition to your password, or any number of other 2-factor solutions. Although 2FA is not immune to compromise, and there've been some high-profile examples of where 2FA systems were hacked, it is hugely more secure than single factor (password only) authentication.

If the system that you are using offers you 2-factor Authentication, then my commendation is to avail of it. It makes your login process slightly more cumbersome, but adds an additional layer of security that might be important to you.

Safety Tip #4: Check to see is your account has been compromised in a data breach (referred to as being "pwned"). Visit the website www.haveibeenpwned.com and enter either an email address or a username for any of your online accounts and then press the "pwned?"

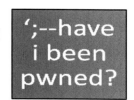

button. If you find that you have been pwned, you need to change all instances of the affected password.

Safety Tip #5: If you have to share passwords (or any other sensitive information) with friends, family or colleagues via electronic communication systems (texting, email or Social Media), always split the information across two different systems. For examples, if you have to send a password to your spouse, send half the password via a text message, and the other half via WhatsApp. That way, only the recipient will get both halves of the password.

Safety Tip #6: Use the Password Rule technique to generate new passwords for all of your accounts.

Safety Tip #7: For each of your accounts, investigate whether Two-factor authentication is available, and if it is, implement it to gain additional peace of mind.

Safety Tip #8: If the above safety tips are not for you, investigate password storage systems. One of the best on the market is LastPass.

9 PREDATORS

The dictionary defines 'predator' as "An animal that lives by capturing and eating other animals.". Predators in the wild - lions, tigers, sharks etc - do not sit around waiting for their dinners to turn up - they actively hunt their prey. That is their nature.

A sexual predator is a person who obtains or tries to obtain sexual contact with another person in a 'predatory' manner. The word 'predator' is not lightly used to describe these individuals - again, like predators in the wild, sexual predators do not sit back hoping for accidental, fortuitous contact with their victims. They are called 'predators' because they actively hunt for their victims. They use any number of techniques to get access to their victims. They are not passive!

At the time of writing, population statistics of the major regions of the world together with Internet usage for each region (in percentage and numbers) are as follows:

Region	Population	% using Internet	Internet Users
Asia	4,478,315,164	45.2%	2,024,198,454
Africa	1,246,504,865	28.3%	352,760,876
Europe	739,207,742	77.4%	572,146,792
Latin America	647,565,336	59.6%	385,948,940
Northern America	363,224,006	88.1%	320,000,349
Oceania / Australia	40,467,040	68.1%	27,558,054

Unfortunately, there are few studies of sexual predators operating on the Internet world wide. However, we can make an educated guess based on studies that are available. Most of these studies are of internet usage in the United States and according to several studies, in the USA at any one time there are between 750,000 to 1 million sexual predators using the Internet to target their victims. If we take say the midpoint of that range, say 850,000 that equates to approximately 0.29% of the Internet-connected population of the USA.

Applying that same percentage to the entire Internet-connected population of the planet, we arrive at a startling figure - 10,679,579. That's ten million predators using the Internet!

I admit, these figures are not robustly checked or vetted. They are indeed simply estimates, but let's be conservative. Let's halve the estimate. That is still five million potential individuals out there hunting our children. And you know what? The truth is, just one predator is one predator too many.

What astounds me most about this, is the lack of understanding displayed by the parents I meet. In the 'old days' - pre-Internet - we, as parents, were very clear on a couple of safety rules for kids: Don't talk to strangers; Don't approach the stranger in a car on the curb; Don't take sweets from a stranger in the park! We even gave it a name - "Stranger Danger".

But when it comes to the biggest, ugliest, most dangerous 'playground' humans have ever invented - the Internet - we've completely forgotten the advice of old - and we regularly abandon our kids without supervision to all of the dangers that the Internet poses.

Types of predatory activity

Predators on the Internet have various goals to their online activities. Some (thankfully they are in the minority), are actively looking for physical contact with our children, whereas others are content with online contact only. Also, there is a category of sexual predators who are referred to as 'browsers' who never make contact with their victims, they simply remain hidden behind fake accounts and 'stalk' their victims - stealing images and information that support their cravings.

In one of his recent radio shows Ryan Tubridy interviewed Lisa[3], a young woman from Cork, Ireland. Lisa was at the time of the interview, a 19-year old student in Cork University. At the time of the interview, she and her friends had just discovered that a group of paedophiles, somewhere on the planet, had stolen all of their images from their social media accounts.

The images were from when the girls were very young. The paedophiles were using these innocent images for their own nefarious purposes. I was aware of this particular crime several years before the Mr. Tubridy's interview, because the same crime had featured twice on the RTE Prime Time Television program aired first on the 4th of December,

---

[3] I've changed her name to protect her privacy

2014[4]. The documentary highlights several practices that will shock parents:

- Predators are 'friending' children and teens under the guise of fake accounts. They are then stealing their images and putting them up on hardcore pornography sites.
- A fake account of a 14-year old girl (fabricated by the programmes journalists and the RTE graphics department) notched up over a thousand 'friend' requests in just thirty days.
- The images that are stolen are largely innocent images of the children simply enjoying themselves - holiday shots, sports shots, party and disco shots etc.
- Often, victims will receive hardcore images from these predators. Remember, your child will believe they are 'friends' with someone of their own age - so will trustingly provide all sorts of personal details to these accounts allowing the perpetrators to get to them.
- Once the images have been stolen and distributed, they will attract the worst sort of online pervert.

Grooming

In some cases (and these cases will often hit the media sooner than other subtler cases), the criminal wants to meet their victims in person and physically 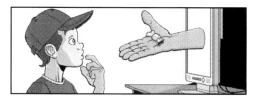 molest them. This is facilitated through a process known as 'grooming'. Youngsters have a different word for it. If you hear your child talking about "catfishing", know that they are referring to the same thing.

Predators setup fake social media accounts. They make these accounts as realistic as possible and they will set up several of them - so that they can simulate normal Social Media activity, by

---

[4] www.rte.ie/news/player/prime-time/2014/1204/

'friending' each of the fake accounts together. Once they have their fake accounts setup and working they send out 'friend' requests to their potential victims. Our children, thoughtlessly accept these random friend requests. You can see how easy it is for predators to get into our children's lives.

Once they are friends with our kids, the Predators will strike up online conversations with their victims. The children think they are chatting to other kids with similar interests to them, and they happily participate in the online chat.

For the most part, the chat is innocent. The predator does not want to scare his victims away. The predator wants to build trust, and is patient in his endeavours.

The conversation - grooming - will go on for as long as necessary. It can be months before anything actually happens. All the time the predator is building trust with his victim.

The predator will glean information from the victim as part of the grooming process. This information will be written down to be used against the victim at a later stage.

When ready, the predator will start to make his move. The conversation will start to subtly change. In essence, three key things will be said to the victim:

- The predator (don't forget that your child will believe they are chatting to a person of their own age - a friend) will suggest that the two of them should meet up. This will be couched in non-threatening language, and will use the information that the predator has gathered about the victim. For example, the victim may have told the so-called friend that she lives in Galway. The predator will say something like "Hey, I'm coming to Galway in a couple of weeks' time with my parents. Why don't we meet up?". *This is the first sign that something is amiss - a request from a stranger online to meet up in real life.*

- The conversation will progress and the predator will eventually offer the victim a gift of some sort. It might go as follows: "Why don't we meet at the cinema - I already have tickets to the xyz movie" or "I have just got back from holidays in Tenerife and I got you a present - I'll bring it along". *This is the second sign that something is amiss - an offer of a gift from a stranger online*

- And lastly the predator, who would obviously not want anyone else involved, will tell the victim to "keep it a secret", "don't tell your parents" or "come alone". *Any time that an online 'friend' suggests that you don't tell anyone else, is a sure sign that things are not right.*

Performance

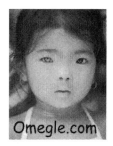

Omegle.com

Video publishing and sharing apps abound. I'm talking here about the apps that facilitate amateur videographers - the budding film stars of the future. There are hundreds of these Apps, probably the most popular are ones like Musical.ly, Omegle, Flipagram, DubSmash, Instagram and Periscope.

These apps all facilitate the recording, editing, production and publishing of home-made videos, and they all have one thing in common - they make the process easy and really fun. The use of such apps is proliferating at an incredible pace and the age of a typical user of these apps is reducing rapidly.

Children love these apps because they can create fun, and funny videos of themselves and their friends - and then can publish them and get followers. Kids don't call them 'followers' but are more inclined to refer to their followers as 'fans'. That is key to understanding the central motivator for the kids - with a few clicks of a button they can quickly feel like a celebrity. You'll find kids as young as 8 comparing their numbers of 'fans'!

Predators know all of this and realise that with a little effort, they can access millions of potential targets - simply by setting up fake accounts on these platforms and then becoming 'fans' of the performers. And here's the real danger, so-called 'fans' can communicate with the 'performer'. There is a growing number of 'performers' who will do whatever their fans ask for. As mentioned earlier in the book, as much as 30% of online child pornography, *is created by the victim*! This is how it happens. A kid is innocently posting dancing videos of themselves onto say Flipagram, and a 'fan' will request that they do something a little 'naughty'. The child, who is probably alone in their bedroom, cannot see the harm in this - so they oblige. The next request from the 'fan' will be a little more extreme and so on.

Who are the Predators?

There is no easy way of spotting a Sexual Predator in real life! They come from every walk of life, every socio-economic grouping, every profession, rich or poor. Earlier, I talked about anonymity and the Internet. Once a person feels completely anonymous, all social norms disappear and what is left is an individual's base instincts and personal moral compass. The Sexual Predator who your child meets on the Internet under the guise of say a Social Media account set up to look like a child, could as easily be the unemployed alcoholic who lives across the Atlantic, as they could be the chartered accountant who lives on the same street as you and helps out with the local scouting group. If we've learnt nothing else about humans since the advent of the Internet, we have learned this - humans can lead multiple, secret lives and the Internet has empowered millions of individuals to do just this.

The vast majority of child-molesters are male but you cannot discount the fact that females commit child sexual abuse as well.

Girls are more frequently the victims of child sexual abuse, but not by a huge margin.

In around 40% of cases where the victim is under the age of 6, the perpetrator is themselves a juvenile.

Safety Tip #1: Do not EVER let your kids use the Internet in private and unsupervised. You need to get Internet Access out of the bedroom and ensure that your children can only access the Internet when there are other people (adults) present.

Safety Tip #2: Make sure your children know the three signs of grooming:
1. *a request to meet in real life*;
2.*an offer of a present* and
3. *a request to keep it secret.*

If any of these elements are present in an online conversation, your child should report it immediately. Also, you need to regularly remind you kids of these signs and point out to them that the words used won't be the same - it's the underlying meaning of the words that is important.

Safety Tip #3: NOTE: THIS IS NOT FOR THE FAINT HEARTED. There are hundreds of references to Omegle on YouTube. Many of them are individuals trying to catch predators out. Simply type in "Omegle" into YouTube and you'll find them. A Channel worth looking at is called "Catching Creeps" and a video worth looking at is called "Omegle Child Predator".

10 PORNOGRAPHY

(The "NSFW" in the graphic above, stands for "Not Safe for Work")

Pornography - are we obsessed?

Whether we choose to ignore the fact or not, all kids, at some stage during their development towards adulthood, will become curious and seek out pornography on the Internet.

Let's be honest, if the internet had been invented when we were in our teenage years, we probably would have as well! The closest our generation ever got to pornography was perhaps the odd book or pornographic magazine.

Try to recall how difficult it was for you, as a young curious teenager, to view a pornographic image. I want you to contrast your experience with just how easy it is today.

Have you ever sat down with your family to watch the latest movie release on a web streaming service only to discover that the website was full of pornographic advertisements and pop ups? It is very common nowadays to stumble across inappropriate content, in particular porn, even when you are not looking for it!

Our kids can view just about anything online within a few clicks. It's not just pornography that our kids can easily access, it's any type of inappropriate content that is available on the internet (graphic images from car crashes, be-headings, animal cruelty, violence, gang rape) I could go on.

The internet is basically a huge 'library' of content, ready and easily accessible to young curious minds. Once you buy your child their first phone or even hand your young son or daughter a tablet or phone, you need to be very aware of how powerful the device is and you also need to take responsibility for whatever they get up to, either accidentally or otherwise.

Unfortunately, pornography has become far more 'acceptable' as part of peoples' lives nowadays, in particular with your child's generation. Over the years I have worked with young teens in a number of different organisations and I am often shocked by how easily pornography is shared between teens (in particular teenage boys).

The fact that porn is so widely available to our children poses a wide range of questions:

- Does viewing pornography create a different level of expectation between teenage couples?

- What sort of effect will the ease at which porn is readily available have on their attitudes towards the opposite sex?

- Will they carry this attitude later into life as they settle down with their spouses?

- Will this manifest itself in the relationships that their own children will have in the future?

- Have today's young teens less morals than our generation as a result?

- Is a person's private life and their attitude towards privacy slowly being eroded away?

- Are teens becoming more narcissistic as they develop their on-line profiles?

These are all questions that we as a society can ask but to which we don't have the answer. There are far more questions than answers I'm afraid. Previous generations in the past have never been as totally surrounded by technology (or pornography) as our children's generation. There is no template to show us what effects this will have on people in the coming years. There are no alarm bells going off at Government level to put strong controls in place to help prevent easy access to pornography by our kids.

That really brings me back to my opening sentence. Whether you are aware of it or not (and let's be realistic here, they are hardly going to tell you) our kids & teens are currently accessing an unhealthy amount of porn. We have established that there are no real controls in place, either at Government level or from the industry itself. So where does that leave us? The responsibility to impose some sort of controls lies with us the parents. We have outlined in chapter 13 how to put router controls in place so at least the majority of inappropriate content is filtered out in the home. It is much more difficult, but not impossible to put controls on a teenager's phone. Most teens now are very quick to argue the case for unlimited broadband when setting up their phone package. Others are very quick to take advantage of free Wifi which is becoming more and more available in public places. So, it appears that outside of the home is the potential danger area for kids. A regular spot check on your kid's phone, not allowing phones during sleep or study time, checking browsing history and warning your kids of the dangers of posting their entire lives on-line can all help. I have also listed some additional safety tips below which may also be of some help.

What is Virtual Reality?

The definition of Virtual Reality is "the computer-generated simulation of a three-dimensional image or environment that can be interacted with in a seemingly real or physical way by a person using special electronic equipment, such as a helmet with a screen inside or gloves fitted with sensors. The person becomes part of this virtual world or is immersed within this environment and whilst there, is able to manipulate objects or perform a series of actions."

You might not be familiar with Virtual Reality but I can guarantee that your kids are!

Now try to imagine a combination of this virtual technology and pornography. Virtual reality porn has been described as is the next great porn frontier and is showing very alarming growth figures.

 Raymond Wong is a Senior Tech Correspondent at mashable.com. He reviews gadgets and tech toys and analyses the tech industry. He writes "after trying out VR porn, I don't think anyone who experiences it will be able to go back to 2D porn. It's that realistic". Virtual Reality is a form of technology that is here to stay. Our present world is full of what is known as Artificial Narrow Intelligence and when we consider that Artificial General Intelligence and Artificial Super Intelligence are the next progressive steps in Artificial Intelligence development, the mind boggles as to where this will take us in the next 20 years!

Some interesting facts about the pornographic industry:

It is very difficult to put a figure on the revenues generated annually by the porn industry and as David Klatell, Associate Dean of the Columbia Graduate School of Journalism notes, "[Pornography] is an industry where they exaggerate the size of everything."

Globally, porn is reported to be a $97 billion-dollar industry, according to Kassia Wosick, assistant Professor of Sociology at New Mexico State University. At present, between $10 and $12 billion of that comes from the United States. It is very difficult to verify the figures but one thing is for certain, it's a huge industry and it's not going anywhere!

- It is estimated that 12 % of all internet content is of a pornographic nature

- It is also estimated that 30% of all child pornography is now self-produced – that means that children & teenagers are filming themselves and the result ends up on the Internet.

- PornHub and XVideo, at the time of writing, are worth $2.5 billion and $3 billion respectively. In fact, XVideo, on its own, is bigger than Dropbox, CNN and New York Times combined.

- XVideo is almost as big as Netflix and gets almost as many page-views every day, both getting more or less 3 billion page views each day.

- Mind Geek, who owns PornHub, Brazzers, YouPorn and Reality Kings, is one of the top 3 bandwidth-consuming companies in the world, the other two being Google and Netflix. This is not surprising when you realize that every second, more than 30 million people are watching some sort of pornographic content.

- Hollywood releases approximately 600 movies and makes $10 billion in profit every year while the porn industry releases 13,000 films and generates close to $15 billion in profit.

- In the US, the porn industry makes more money than Major League Baseball, The National Football League and The NBA combined.

Software solutions for filtering out content (Parental Control Software):

There are many software solutions available that are designed to give parents control of the content that their children have access and, indeed, to give control to the parents over every aspect of their children's online lives.

There are too many to list here, but those listed below are the more popular and well-known solutions.

These systems allow you to set up an online account, and then through the use of an App installed on your children's devices, control what they are doing. Three basics of most of the systems are:

1. You can set levels of filters for the content they can view;
2. You can put in schedules for the time your children can use their devices; and
3. the system will provide you with regular reports on your children's screen-based activity.

According to the toptenreviews.com website, the 9 top Parental Control Software solutions are:

1. Qustodio ($49.95)
2. Norton Family ($49.99)
3. Surfie ($39.90)
4. Net Nanny ($39.99)
5. Witigo ($49.99)
6. SpyAgent ($69.99)
7. ContentBarrier ($39.99)
8. WebWatcher ($99.95)
9. Verity ($49.99)

If you are looking for a free solution then try out Windows Live Family Safety – by Microsoft. This is completely free and very powerful. One major drawback is that it only works on Windows-based devices.

See Chapter 13 for similar controls you can put in place using your home Wifi router.

11 THE DEEP WEB, THE DARK WEB

You might have heard of The Deep Web, The Invisible Web, or the Hidden Web. You might well have heard of the Surface Web, or the Visible Web and indeed you might have also heard of the Dark Web or Dark Net. You would be forgiven for being utterly confused, and feeling at least a little fearful of these sinister terms. I'm going to try and clear up the confusion, however I am not attempting here to provide you with a fully peer-reviewed academic look at it. This chapter is designed to enlighten you a little bit so that you can understand something of what your children might be exploring in this realm of the dark-arts! And you do need to be informed. In the last 18 months, I have noticed during my talks to both primary and secondary school children, a marked increase in the number of questions I get about the Deep Web. There is a mystique surrounding the Deep Web and children, being naturally curious, are starting to explore it. You CANNOT allow you kids to explore the Deep Web

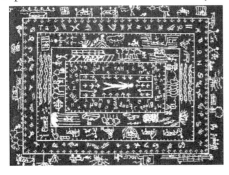

without your knowledge or supervision.

We need to start at the beginning - the Internet. Remember in Chapter 1? I defined the Internet as the physical network of interconnected computers blanketing the globe. Every website, every email, every Social Media message, every video etc. uses the physical network called the **Internet**.[5] There are several 'information spaces' that use the Internet. The **World Wide Web** (or www for short) is one such 'information space', where documents and other web resources are distributed using the Internet.

The **Deep Web** on the other hand is the part or subset of the World Wide Web which cannot be indexed by standard search engines like Google. Content on the Deep Web is hidden from view - where 'view' means hidden from normal search engines. Examples of very common uses of the Deep Web would be online banking and encrypted, confidential email systems.

And then there is the **Dark Web** which is content that exists on what are called **Darknets**. Darknets are *overlay networks* that exist on the Internet and that require special hardware or software and/or configurations to access. There are two types of Darknet - there are peer-to-peer darknets, that allow individuals to share files without going through central servers, and then there are the 'privacy' darknets, the most famous one being TOR (The Onion Router) where you need the Tor Browser to access it, and where most sites would be 'onion' sites - a reference to the top-level domain name 'onion'.

Not everything on the Dark Web is bad. Indeed, there are many aspects of the Dark Web that are good. Whistle-blower sites use the Dark Web to protect the identity of whistle-blowers. Several main-stream newspapers provide Dark Web versions of their publications so that people in oppressed societies can avail of news without fear of persecution. The Dark Web provides anonymity, which is a good thing - you really don't want the government or big-business monitoring your everyday online and offline activities. However, the Dark Web provides the same anonymity to everyone - good and bad alike. Illegal activities thrive on

---

[5] Infographic depicting the layers of the Internet. The centre of this is referred to as the Mariana Web - named after the Mariana Trench - the deepest point of the ocean.

the Dark Web.

If your children are exploring the Dark Web unsupervised, they will find the worst of the worst content imaginable! The Dark Web - for all of its protection of privacy and anonymity - is the haven of the worst that humanity has to offer.

Safety Tip #1: Look out for the Tor Browser on your children's devices. This is the most popular software for accessing the content on the Deep Web and therefore is the application of choice for anyone wanting to access the Dark Web. If your child has downloaded TOR then you can be fairly certain they've started to explore the Dark Web.

 Safety Tip #2: Check to see if your children are using Torrent apps. "Torrents" are a clever way to download large files like movies, games, and TV shows. They turn your computer into part of a 'swarm' where information is shared as it's downloaded - so while you're downloading something from other people you're also helping others download the bits you've already got. The result is a very reliable and often very fast way to get your hands on huge files. The problem with torrents is threefold: firstly, in most instances it is illegal to download commercial content this way - you are breaking copyright law and also depriving the creator of the revenue that they are entitled to; secondly, for every 'real' torrent, there are dozens of fake torrents which contain viruses and malware. Unless your children are very careful - they can easily accidentally download malware onto their devices; and lastly, torrents are extensively used to distribute pornography (including illegal material). You should look for torrent clients on your children's devices. 5 of the most popular Torrent Clients are:

- qBittorrent
- Deluge
- uTorrent
- BitTorrent
- Vuze

12 INTERNET CHALLENGES

For all the advantages that the Internet offers, there are as many worrying elements, particularly for parents. An 'Internet Challenge' certainly falls into this category. Internet Challenges have taken on a life of their own in recent years. While some of the challenges range from mildly amusing to downright hilarious, there are many that result in either serious injury or even loss of life.

What is an Internet Challenge?

A challenge usually features an Internet user (or a group of people) recording themselves carrying out a challenge. They then distribute the result through social media sites, often challenging / daring / inspiring others to repeat the challenge.

Not all challenges are harmful. Some challenges have resulted in hundreds of thousands being raised for various charities around the world. One of the most famous of these was the Ice Bucket Challenge which swept through the Internet in 2015/2016.

This fun challenge involved a person nominating three other

people to either donate a sum of money to a chosen charity or else to record themselves pouring a bucket of ice-cold water over their heads. If they decided to choose the latter option the person could make a smaller donation to the chosen charity and challenge three others with the same challenge via social media. As the challenge grew in popularity, celebrities from all over the world became involved. Their large social media following helped to make the challenge go viral.

Challenges to be wary of:

Some of the more sinister challenges on the Internet, although every bit as popular, are not always as kind to those who are challenged. Some of the more popular challenges in the recent past are listed below.

- **The Blue Whale Challenge** – Earlier this year (2017) a 14-year-old Irish boy in a town on the west coast of Ireland, committed suicide. It is believed that he was participating the Blue Whale Challenge. I regularly give talks to the schools in this town and the incident profoundly affected the people of the area. The challenge purportedly started in Russia (and has been linked to several teenage suicides in Russia). It gets its name from a reference to a phenomenon in which the Blue Whale strands itself on land, typically leading to its death. The 'game' consists of a series 50 daily tasks (or challenges) provided by a so-called "curator". The tasks start off simply and are reasonably benign (for example "Watch a scary movie") but over the 50 days become more and more extreme, involving self-mutilation, harming others and on the 50th day – committing suicide. The 'player' has to video or photograph each task and publish it on social media.

- **The Cinnamon Challenge** was one of the most popular challenges in the last number of years. The 'player' had to film themselves eating a spoonful of ground cinnamon in under a minute without taking a drink and then upload the video to the Internet. This particular challenge can cause serious health risks as the

93

cinnamon coats and dries both the mouth and throat. This results in coughing, gagging, vomiting and breathing in the cinnamon, which can lead to throat irritation, breathing difficulties, and even risk of pneumonia or a collapsed lung.

- **The Kylie Jenner Challenge** – This challenge tried to get the Internet User to recreate the puffy lips of US television star Kylie Jenner, Internet users show themselves using a small vessel like a shot glass that covers their lips, drawing all the air out of the 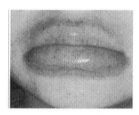 vessel, and then releasing, which temporarily puffs the lips by drawing the user's blood into them. The activity is considered harmful, both from bruising and dis-figuration of the lips, and the potential for the vessel to shatter and cut the person".

- **The Salt & Ice Challenge** – This Internet Challenge first appeared in 2016 and 'players' are dared to pour salt on their skin, (usually on an arm). Ice is then poured on the salt which causes a burning sensation. The challenge is to withstand the pain for as long as possible while being recorded. The result is then posted on social media.

- **The Choking Challenge** – This particularly worrying game involves one person using their weight or a tight hold causing strangulation. This reduces oxygen to the brain, causing the participant to faint while being filmed and posted on-line. This social media challenge has also resulted in a number of deaths.

- **Food challenges** – There are many variations of food challenges which have surfaced over the years. Most involve the 'player' filming themselves eating various types of foods, (very hot / spicy, disgusting, indigestible, etc), with all kinds of results experienced, from vomiting to hospitalization.

- **The Charlie Charlie Challenge** – This challenge involves the use of a Ouija type setting where two pencils are used to point to a 'Yes' or 'No' answer. A fictitious demon called  'Charlie' is called upon to answer questions posed by the user or group.

- **The Fire Challenge** – This was a particular horrific challenge as the 'player' was challenged to pour flammable liquid over a part of their body and set fire to the liquid while filming themselves. This challenge often resulted in severe burns and has been attributed to a number of deaths in the past.

- **The Condom Challenge** – This challenge meant that the person had to insert a condom into the nasal cavity before inhaling it through their nose and cough it out through the mouth.

- **Butt chugging/eyeballing** - Instead of drinking alcohol, some teens are ingesting their alcohol through their rectum in an effort to become intoxicated. Butt chugging is extremely dangerous and can cause severe  alcohol poisoning, tissue damage and death. Eyeballing is an equally disturbing teen trend that involves downing a shot of alcohol through the eye socket. Eyeballing can cause irritation, swelling, cornea scarring and blindness. Some teen girls are soaking tampons in vodka and other hard alcohol and inserting them in the same manner they would a regular tampon.

The challenges listed above give you, as a parent, some idea of the difficulty that each one poses. The particular ones I have chosen as examples represent just some of the hundreds of different challenges that circulate the internet and raise curiosity in our children from time to time. For every challenge that dies away with the passage of time, a new challenge grows in popularity with its origins in some remote corner of the world.

There are many other Challenges that are out there on the Internet some of which are:

- o The Eat It or Wear It Challenge
- o Disney Challenge.
- o Try Not to Laugh Challenge
- o Innuendo Bingo
- o The Whisper Challenge
- o Say Anything Challenge
- o Bean Boozled Challenge
- o Touch my Body
- o Chubby Bunny
- o Speed drawing
- o The Duct Tape Challenge

The real challenge is for us parents to keep our children safe while using the Internet and 'Challenges' are another obstacle in our way.

It is hard for us as parents to understand why ordinary, well behaved teens succumb so easily to an Internet Challenge, (particularly those which have a dangerous or horrific outcome). A teens brain works differently to that of an adult. Their lack of a 'Sense of Danger' blinds them into seeing only the fun side of life at times. Most of the Challenges on the Internet are either portrayed as great fun or the peer pressure element can also be a major factor in a teen agreeing to a new exciting challenge.

Many accept and then post these challenges on to their friends in the hope of becoming more popular, getting more likes or even hoping to be the next internet sensation.

Others are merely trying to be accepted, included in certain social circles or have their challenge re-posted by their social media followers.

Safety Tip #1: As a parent, you never envisage having to teach your child not to inhale a teaspoon of cinnamon or to avoid setting themselves on fire, but I'm afraid in today's technology rich era, it seems that is a conversation we are destined to have!

Safety Tip #2: We can't really prevent our teenagers from coming across these Internet Challenges. By the time we hear about it, the challenge has usually reached viral status which makes it impossible to remove from the Internet.
However, we can teach them to stop and think for themselves before they participate in the latest challenge doing the rounds.

Safety Tip #3: It is always best to keep the lines of communication open and discuss the long-term effects of these challenges with your child. Have a conversation around the influence of peer pressure and the value of saying 'No' when necessary.

Safety Tip #4: If you become aware that your child is showing an interest in a particular Internet Challenge, you need to act quickly. Find out more about it by researching it on the Internet yourself.

Safety Tip #5: Educate yourself on the outcomes of the Challenge and sit with your child and explain the dangers to them.

Safety Tip #6: Social Media channels will facilitate the deletion of inappropriate content, either voluntarily or if brought to their attention.

Safety Tip #7: Warn your child about NOT following trends without first talking to you (e.g. 'challenges')

13 THE IMPORTANT ROLE A HOME ROUTER PLAYS

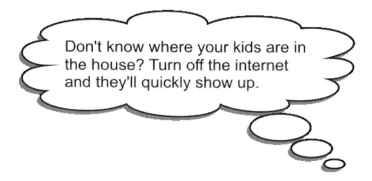

A quick warning: There are hundreds of different brands, types and models of home router available. I cannot possibly give the details for all of them in this book. You will need to do a bit of further research for the router you actually have in your house.

In this chapter, I will talk about the importance of the Home Router and show you the steps involved in setting it up. I will also look at setting up some of the more important controls that you need to put in place.

1. How to set up a Home Router and schedule the Wifi

If you don't already have one, it is always best to get a router that allows content filtering.

A Content Filtering router will allow you to set a number of different restrictions on the broadband as it enters your home and prior to its distribution to the various devices connected to it throughout the house (e.g. tablet, laptop, smartphone, etc).

Like with most purchases you make in life, in general the more you pay, the better the quality or spec of the product that you get. You can spend any amount on a router but I would advise against going for the cheapest on the market as it will not have the functionality that you will need. Talk to someone in the store who knows about routers and tell them you would like the following features:

- The ability to schedule the Wifi
- The ability to easily change the Wifi password
- The ability to filter out inappropriate content (if this is carried out automatically by the router then all the better)
- The ability to block random websites or Social Media platforms if necessary
- The ability to have different schedules for different devices.

When you get home, plug in the router and then the broadband cable (from your broadband supplier) into the WAN port. This port is often set a little to the side and away from the other ports and may even be a different colour to the other ports.

You will need at least one device connected to the router, either via Ethernet cable or via Wifi, in order to adjust the settings on your new router. Once the router is physically set up you should then log in to the router itself by following the manufacturer's instructions, (every router has its own built in, internal website where you can carry out a range of useful functions). To do this, open an Internet browser on your device and in the address bar of the browser (not Google!) type in the web address of the router's internal website. For NETGEAR routers this is "routerlogin.net". For LINKSYS routers use the web address "192.168.1.1" (for all others the web address is probably written on the sticker on the bottom of the router).

Once you are logged in you will have the ability to:

- Set a new router login password
- Schedule a time for the broadband to be disabled to all devices or some devices, e.g. night time
- Schedule a time for the broadband to be enabled to all devices or some devices, e.g. morning time
- Block access to any number of selected websites
- Block access to the internet using certain keywords – the more keywords that are identified the greater the restriction

The illustration above shows a typical menu system for a Linksys router. Again because of the huge range of routers on the market, you

will need to study the menu options and also reference the start-up guide for help.

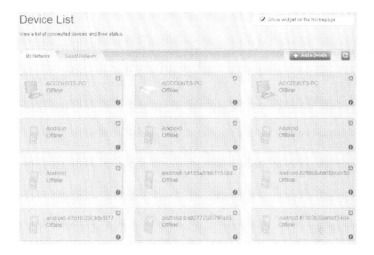

The device list above shows you the list of devices that connect to the router and will give you their current status, (i.e. off-line or on-line). It should be possible to edit the name of each device to make it easier for you to see who is using the internet at any given time. The area that we will now focus on is the Parental Controls section (see below):

Once you click in to this, on most routers, you should be able to carry out a full range of functions on each device.

The menu below is from my own home Linksys Router and is typical of a well laid out menu system, found on most good routers.

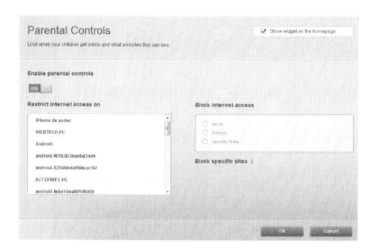

If I select a particular phone, I then have the option to decide whether to:

1) Never block Internet Access
2) Always block Internet Access
3) Block Internet Access during specific times

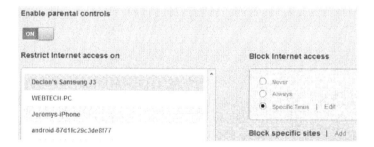

By choosing the 'Specific Times' function, if I click on 'Edit', it opens up a schedule that I can edit. This allows me to turn off and on the Wifi at specific times throughout the week. This allows you to turn off the Wifi at say 9pm on a week night but perhaps turn it off at a later time on a Friday & Saturday night for slightly older children in the house, (see below).

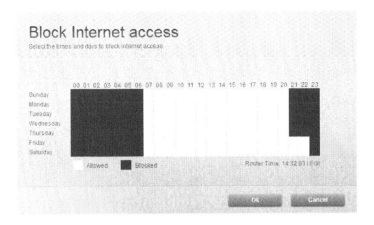

This type of schedule is common on routers with parental controls and as you can see, allows you to block Internet at 60-minute intervals.

You may also want to block specific sites or Social Media Platforms that you do not wish your kids to visit. Most routers have this functionality within the 'Parental Controls' section, (see below):

To add a particular site to the 'banned sites' list, simply click on the 'Add' button and enter the website domain into the box as per the illustration below:

Block specific sites |

Enter a website to block

2. How to change the Wifi & Router passwords

On my own particular router, it is possible to change both the Wifi password and the Router Admin password in the 'Connectivity' menu. On some systems, it may well be located in the 'Security' section or elsewhere. Refer to the Router handbook if you are having difficulty finding it.

Bear in mind the difference between the 'Router' Admin password and the 'Wifi' password.

The 'Router' Admin password is the password that you will need anytime you want to log into the router internal website itself. This is a very important password and under no circumstances should your children know this password. At the start of the book, I have provided space for recording the login credentials for your Home Router. If you use this book to log the details make sure to keep it in a safe place and away from prying eyes at all times!

The 'Wifi' password is the password needed by any device within the home, to connect to the Internet. The Wifi password is the password that your kids will give to their friends when they call around to your house. It is good practice to change the Wifi password on a regular basis before everyone in the neighbourhood becomes familiar with it and uses it without your knowledge. It never ceases to amaze me during my visits to Primary Schools (in particular), just how many do not have any password on their school Wifi. I can remember one Principal who was a little surprised by my concern but said it may explain the number of cars parked in the school car park each evening! Imagine the consequences of having to explain to the authorities if the school broadband was ever used to download illegal material!

It is always worth putting a strong password on any Wifi, (home, school or business). I have given you tips on how to set a strong password in Chapter 8 of this book.

To change the Wifi password, click on the 'Connectivity' menu and use the edit button to change the default password.

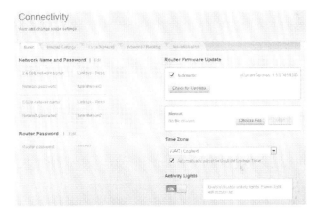

To change the 'Router' password, again click on the edit button and follow the steps provided.

What is an Ikydz Router?

My own Home router is a little more advanced than most as it comes with its own Linksys App. This App has allowed me in the past to log in remotely to my router and make some basic changes to the schedule, see the devices connected and turn on or off the Wifi as I needed to. This was all very useful on various occasions and gave me some control over the Home Wifi whenever I was working remotely. My own experience was that it was not always reliable and the App would sometimes crash.

I recently purchased an iKydz router as I was looking for something a little simpler and more reliable to operate. The iKydz website lists the following as the main features:

Age-based restrictions - Apply age-based restrictions to your kids' internet connected devices with one easy click. You wouldn't want your 6-year-old seeing things that your 15-year-old is allowed to watch. So, use our standard age-based restrictions to give you peace of mind.

Block apps - Use the standard blocks to prevent or limit access to social media, chat rooms or other apps, such as Instagram, Facebook, Yellow, Simsimi, Tinder, WhatsApp and a host of others.

Block Websites - Use the iKydz Global Block Lists to block content such as Adult, Gaming, Violence & Gambling.

Block Pop-ups - Stop inappropriate pop-ups from appearing on your kids' screens when they browse the web or look at YouTube.

Filter Content - Apply suitable internet content filters to individual devices based on the age of your child.

Monitor Internet Use - Monitor how long your kids spend online and what they spend their time viewing using the Reporting tool.

Schedule Online Access - Easily set daily or weekly schedules for when your children are allowed to be online.

Shut off the Internet - Use the Mealtime button to give your kids a break from the Internet; shuts down for 30 minutes and then it automatically turns back on.

All things considered, this is quite an impressive list of features and basically it does what it says on the tin!

The great thing about an iKydz router is that it will connect to your existing router and turn it into the type of router that every household needs.

*It allows you the parent to determine when and how your children access the Internet. You decide which devices, (phones, tablets, games consoles) can be used, so that each child has a unique tailored experience that is consistent with your family 'rules' for how the Internet is used in your home.

How to set up an iKydz Router

When you purchase an iKydz router, in the box you will find:

- The iKydz controller unit
- A power adaptor
- A network cable
- The step by step guide to getting started

Plug in the iKydz controller and connect it to the LAN/Ethernet port on the back of your Wifi router using the cable provided. This sets up the IKYDZ network in your home.

One-time Registration

In order to be able to manage the iKydz network in your home, you must register with iKydz so that only you (and not your tech-savvy children) can determine how it is used.

- On your home PC/laptop/tablet, connect wirelessly to the IKYDZ network, (by clicking on the Network and Sharing Centre in the taskbar of your PC or laptop).
- Connect to the iKydz Network and you will then be asked to enter a password.
- Enter the password **ikydzWifi**, (bear in mind it can take up to 60 seconds to fully connect the first time).
- Open up your browser (Internet Explorer/Mozilla/Chrome/Safari – depending on what device you are using) and type into the URL/address bar: 10.10.10.1.

- Press Enter and you will be taken to the iKydz registration page
- Fill in the fields, read/accept the Terms and Conditions, and press "Begin Registration".
- An on-screen prompt will appear while iKydz downloads to the unit and configures your safe network. Note: this will take up to 10 minutes to install and configure, depending on your broadband speed.

- During this process, any device connected to the iKydz network will have no internet access.
- N.B. DO NOT switch off the iKydz unit during this process.

Setting up iKydz

- Once the iKydz unit has completed its downloads and configuration, connect your own Smartphone to the IKYDZ network and check that all functions are operational and that you can access/surf the Internet as normal.

- Disconnect your children's devices from the existing network by selecting "FORGET" in Wifi settings, and connect them to the secure IKYDZ network (password is ikydzWifi).
- If you have not already done so, using your own Smartphone, download the iKydz app from the Apple Store (iPhones) or the Google Play Store (Android Phones).
- Now you can begin to manage your children's devices on the iKydz network, using either the App on your smartphone or by using the secure private portal

at customerportal.ikydz.com. You can login using the email address and PIN that you used during registration.
- Select each device and set up schedules and block-lists as you wish.
- You are now fully operational on iKydz and in control of your family's Internet access in a safe and secure environment.

Screen shots from the iKydz smartphone app above

One Last Step

We strongly recommend that you change the router and Wifi password on the existing home network. This will prevent your children from using this network – remember you want to ensure that they only use the IKYDZ network to access the Internet.

To change the password, you must log on to your Router, (for a guide on how to change the router password please refer to the earlier section of this paragraph).

You will have received instructions on how to do this from your Internet Service Provider (ISP) when your router was originally installed. If you do not have these, we recommend you go to the manufacturer's website, e.g. Huawei, Netgear, CISCO, Belkin, etc. and follow their instructions.

You will also find instructions on Google, YouTube – search for Changing Router Password. Alternatively, you should contact your ISP who will assist you with this process.

Remember to keep a record of this new password for future reference, (use the 'My Details' section of this book to record all home device passwords).

Now, disconnect your own Smartphone from the IKYDZ network and reconnect it to the existing network, using the new password you have just set up.

Further Support

Please visit the iKydz website at www.ikydz.com where you will find how-to videos and FAQ's in the support section.

Safety Tip #1: When setting up the iKydz router in the home, tell your child in advance and involve them in the process. Discuss the sites / social media platforms that you intend to block and your reasons why. They may even be able to suggest a few that you have never heard of!

Safety Tip #2: Involve your child in the setting up of the Wifi schedule. Reach an agreement on the time the Wifi shuts down for them during the week and give them a bit of extra leeway at the weekends and during holiday periods. If they know in advance, you won't be in the bad books when the Wifi suddenly shuts down on them!

Safety Tip #3: Remember that most social media platforms have a minimum recommended age. This should be used as a guide only and you know your child best. You wouldn't let your child wander the streets alone at night so you should apply the same type of rule when it comes to browsing the Internet and using Social Media.

14 BIG BROTHER IS INDEED WATCHING YOU!

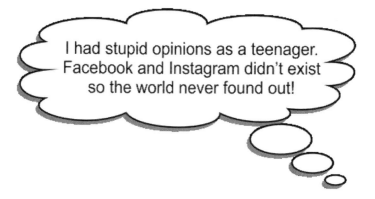

I had stupid opinions as a teenager. Facebook and Instagram didn't exist so the world never found out!

Ever heard of "Big Data"? A couple of years ago I attended a lecture on "Big Data" at NUIG (National University of Ireland Galway). It was entertaining to see the speakers so animated about Big Data - but I have to confess - I came away more confused than when I went in! The problem was that in a new science at that stage, and I didn't have the prerequisite background to really grasp the concepts. Fast forward to now - and I finally get it!

There is "Big Data" and "Little Data". I recently returned home from a much-needed summer holiday. My family and I came back via Dublin airport. After passing through passport control (where the customs official was entirely polite and a delight to deal with) we passed one of those customer survey panels - you've probably seen them yourselves. It's a plinth sitting in an obvious and easily accessible location (probably right in your path) on top of which are four large buttons with faces on them. On the left is a very sad and frowny looking face  and on the right a very smiley, laughy sort of face. The buttons in between progress from sad to happy - the idea being that as you pass by you simply smack the button that best represents your experience as a customer - or in my case, my experience as a person entering the country through the airport. Above the plinth in Dublin airport was a large poster - bragging that the airport had had 1.4 million responses this year. That is "Big Data". From the data gathered by the device, the managers of the airport can glean a lot of information about the crowds that flow through the airport. They can see very quickly which of the four buttons are pressed - thus giving them a general idea of how their airport systems are impacting on the emotional wellbeing of the travellers. They might even be able to check if there are particular times of the day when travellers are more happy or sad. Indeed, they will probably be able to tell if there are certain months in the year where travellers are more content. They won't however be able to tell whether men are more likely to press a button than women - or whether children have a habit of pressing multiple buttons - thus skewing the results. And they certainly won't be able to see if I personally had a happy or sad experience. That sort of information requires something that the customer survey plinth cannot provide. It requires "Small Data".

"Small Data" is data about me - the individual. If I had been asked to participate in a written survey about my experience going through Dublin airport and had provided personal details - number in my party, ages and gender breakdown of the party, and most importantly my contact details, that is Small Data and is very different from Big Data. However, the Big Data  of the plinth example, could quite easily be turned into Small Data by adding a couple of extra measures. By looking at the button presses of people and then mapping them against the duty roster of the customs officials - dips and peaks in customer satisfaction might well be tied to an individual employee's attitude, mood, performance etc. Over time, Big Data/Small Data might show patterns in customer satisfaction that could highlight personnel issues for HR to deal with.

Whether you like it or not, you are already victim of Big Data/Small Data manipulation and you probably aren't aware of it.

Did you know that Google tracks your every search? Did you know that Facebook can track your phone usage (the apps you use and your habits) *even if you don't use Facebook?*

Did you know that Roomba - a very popular robotic vacuum cleaner, maps your house and the company (iRobot) is talking about selling maps of the inside of people's homes to the highest bidder?

Did you know that your smartphone is listening to you, and selling keywords taken from your spoken conversations on to advertisers? Did you know that Google can track your spending habits - *even if you don't buy anything online?*

All of the above cases are examples of artificial intelligence. Humans are not sitting behind the technology actively monitoring you! Artificial intelligence is already here and is already in your life:

- Have you noticed how people are more and more likely to be talking *to* their phones instead of *on* their phones? They are talking to the AI on their phone - in the case of Apple, that would-be 'Siri'; in the case of Android the AI is called Google Now. On Windows devices - it's called Cortána.

- Have you noticed that Gmail is making better suggestions about who to include or exclude from messages? Indeed, have you noticed that your smartphone is making better suggestions for auto-replying to emails and text messages? Again - AI.

- When I'm on the road (and I'm on the road a lot for work), my phone seems to have learned my driving habits and even my work habits. Before I even get into my car, the phone has told me the traffic conditions and the estimated time to my next appointment. Just before I'm about to finish my appointment, my phone gives me a gentle reminder of where I parked my car, and lets me know - very politely I might say -

how long my homeward journey will take.

- A university in Australia has created an AI system that, in 70% of cases, can accurately predict when you're going to die!

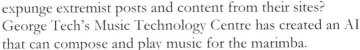

- Did you know that Facebook and Google and other Social Media platforms (SnapChat, Instagram etc.) have developed AIs that can find and expunge extremist posts and content from their sites?
- George Tech's Music Technology Centre has created an AI that can compose and play music for the marimba.

You might still be wondering what the fuss is about. Isn't all of this really exciting? Isn't it going to improve our lives? No doubt, it will, but my concern, on that is shared by many others, is that the big social media companies, have simply got too much power and although they are probably well-intentioned, there are NOT many examples in history where individuals who wield enormous power, have used it for the good of mankind! Tristan Harris, former product manager at Google, maintains that our minds have been hijacked by a handful of tech companies:

"A handful of people working at a handful of tech companies steer the thoughts of billions of people every day" says Harris. Let's name the handful of companies shall we: Apple and Google (who design the hardware and operating systems of the devices we all use), Facebook, YouTube, SnapChat and Instagram (where most people spend their time).

The premise behind the word hijacking is that your control you have over your life is being undermined. If you want to maintain control over your instincts, motives, wishes, desires, and life, then you need to expend enormous energy to overcome the pressures of this manipulation.

There is no easy way to stop the companies from doing this. Harris is making efforts to get Social Media companies to fundamentally change their core designs so that humans are in control of their "timelines". However, his efforts are long-term and will not necessarily benefit you or your children. There is only one way of preventing the companies from manipulating us - and that is to disconnect (see Safety Tip #2 below)!

Let me state here that I am not against a 'life on line' and I am not paranoid about my online presence. I do, however, like to be aware of what companies are doing with my data. The unfortunate thing is, once I put my data on line – it is no longer mine.

Safety Tip #1: If you are at all concerned about the level of snooping going on in your digital lives, then you can do something about it: install Ghostery in your browsers and on your mobile devices. Ghostery (www.ghostery.com), blocks all known tracking systems and prevents companies from gathering information about your browsing, buying, viewing, clicking, liking, and other online habits.

Safety Tip #2: I am not suggesting for a minute that we should all disconnect from Social Media. I am suggesting that as parents we need to understand the risks and put boundaries in place for our children (and for ourselves). Here are my suggested boundaries:

- Don't let children below the age of 13, use any of the main social media platforms - e.g. Facebook, SnapChat and Instagram.
- Time-limit your child's use of YouTube and make sure you know what he or she is watching (or indeed posting) on YouTube.
- For teenagers and young adults, impose time limits on their

use of social media.

- Regularly talk to your children about what they are reading and consuming online. Make sure you temper what they are reading online with other sources of information (newspaper, radio, television).
- Make 'screen-free' areas of your home (the bedrooms!).
- Designate 'screen-free' times of the day or week during which other activities are pursued.
- Use your Wifi router to control how your family accesses the internet (see chapter 12 for more details)

15 PRACTICAL PARENTING IDEAS

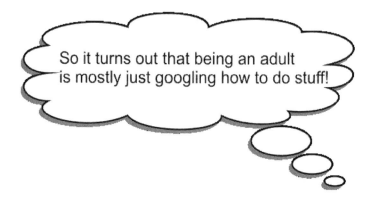

This was probably the simplest chapter to write. We could summarize the entire chapter by reminding you that using old fashioned parenting techniques actually works! The old simple rules still apply even in today's highly technological world:

- Know what your children are doing.
- Talk to your kids.
- Restrict access to certain things at certain times.
- Set the ground rules (and stick to them).
- Monitor their online activity
- Remember you are the Boss!

Nevertheless, we have split the following chapter in to two sections: Section 1 deals with practical parenting ideas for children while Section 2 is for teenagers.

1) Practical Parenting Ideas for children
a) Set up Parental Controls on each Device

All Phones and Tablets have parental controls that enable you to restrict any pre-loaded apps (including YouTube, some Social Media platforms, the device camera, etc). In the Parental Controls section, you can also restrict the ability to downloads apps, prevent the child

from deleting existing helpful apps, block content (e.g. third-party apps and websites), and disable functions such as location services and account settings. Parental controls are usually protected by a PIN or Password, so your child cannot access them.

Remember, to set parental controls on your device, go to: **Settings > General > Restrictions or Security**.

Your device usually presents you with a list of all the apps and functions, so you can decide which to block. It is certainly worth going through the security settings on your device and experimenting which settings suit your own situation best (for example you may wish to block your child from answering any incoming calls, particularly if you have just handed them your work phone!)

All devices have different levels of restrictions and the steps may even vary between different models. It is worth checking the manual for each new device and set up the controls right from the start (phone user manuals can be found online – simply google the make model).

Whether you give your child your device from time to time or purchase their first phone, it is very important to set some ground rules in relation to how much time they get to spend on the device. Have a cut off time at night and stick to it religiously. This can be achieved by taking the device off the child before bedtime or scheduling the Wifi, (see chapter 12) That way it will become the norm and will not be a big issue when the child is in their teens.

If you purchase a phone for your child, you should insist from day one that you have passwords to all of their accounts. This will enable you to carry out occasional spot checks on the various forms of technology they are using. If you don't know the basics of how a particular Social Media platform works (e.g. Snapchat) then you either must teach yourself or get an older sibling, niece or nephew to go through the basics with you. Often your child will show you how to navigate through an app, and this allows you some 'quality' time with your child and gives you an opportunity to ask questions, and then carry out research.

b) Invest in a good protective case for your Phone or Tablet:

It is well worth investing in a strong protective case to keep your phone / tablet / iPad safe from accidental drops, bangs, knocks and spills. A water-resistant case is best but not always the most practical. We all have a tendency to hand over our

precious expensive devices to our children from time to time, even if just to enjoy a quiet moment when you sit down for a cup of tea! Cases made from high quality rubber or polycarbonate are usually the best option to help protect from the accidental damage that occurs at the hands of your children.

c) Lock the device screen

The easiest way to prevent your child from accessing anything on your phone or tablet is to lock your screen. There are a variety of ways to do this (e.g. a PIN or passcode, fingerprint ID, a pattern swipe, etc). That way, if your phone is left unattended, your child will not be able to unlock your phone unless you are present and open the device for them. They will quickly get used to having to come to you to get permission to use the device. A device screen lock can easily be set up in the settings menu of each individual device (look in the security section of the settings).

d) Restrict the child's screen time

There is really is no 'right' age to allow our kids to use today's technology but recommendations are that older children have no more that 1 or 2 hours of screen time per day while children under 2 should be restricted from using screens completely. Screen time refers to any time spent using or in

front of a device (such as a TV, Tablet, Phone, Play Station, etc). It is best to set a rule in your household and this can be tweaked during school holiday periods or at weekends if necessary.

e) Read Permissions on all Apps

This topic has been dealt with in more detail in chapter 4. However, just to recap on the main points:

- Set a rule in the house that your child should always come to you to ask if they can download a new App.
- Check the user reviews of all apps – before installing them for your child
- All apps ask you for permission to access various features of your device. Always read the permissions list BEFORE installing an app.
- If the list requires access to practically everything on your child's phone (including their location), ask yourself does your child really need this game / app?
- Keep your eyes and ears open for information on new apps trending at the moment.
- Talk to your children and make them aware of the dangers of harmful Apps.

f) Teach your child that not everyone they meet online is who they say they are!

There are any number of reports of children who have been lured into a false sense of security, by a paedophile posing as someone their own age and arranging to meet. The outcome is never positive for the victim. It is hard to comprehend how easily this can happen, but it does, and on a regular basis. Remind your child NEVER to friend or meet with anyone they meet on-line and if unsure to talk to you, the parent.

Social media platforms all display the number of likes / friends / streaks / followers that our children have. In our experience, they will often brag about the number of friends or followers they have. It's as if the higher the number the more popular / important they are. Perhaps we have our 'celebrity' culture to thank for this.

Sit with your child and go through their friends / followers periodically and delete or remove anyone they don't actually know. It is also good practice to review the settings on their social media accounts to make sure they are set to private. Often after an update the privacy settings will need to be tweaked.

g) Teach your child never to give out personal details or location online

We are always very concerned by the amount of information that children make publicly available about themselves online. No matter what you sign up to, purchase, look up, download or access, there is always some piece of software collecting details about you. We raise our children to always tell the truth. However, there are some exceptions to this rule, particularly if telling the truth may potentially put your child in danger. Teach your child to always stop and think before parting with any personal details on-line (whether it's a name, a location, a date of birth or your pet's name). Ask yourself why are they gathering this information. Your personal information is very valuable in different ways to different people. A sales & marketing company may pay for your personal information so that they can target products at your age group. A paedophile may want your personal information to try to befriend you and ultimately meet up. A criminal may wish to have as much personal details about you in order to hack your account and steal your money. Whatever the reason, the more information that is available about your child, the more vulnerable they are to be being harmed in some way.

h) Check your child's browsing history

Again, this is one of those tasks that you need do on a regular basis. As with most of our advice, the earlier you start your checks, the better, as they quickly become the norm.

For more details on how to check their browsing history see chapter 15.

Remember, having no browsing history is as concerning as inappropriate browsing history, as your child may have learned how to delete it because they have something to hide! In the device's parental controls, it is possible to change the settings so that the history cannot be deleted. If you find that your child has been searching for inappropriate material, sit with them and have a conversation around why they felt they need to. It will make them aware that you are keeping an eye on them and hopefully embarrass them into not doing it again!

As your child gets older, they will learn how to search in 'Incognito Mode' which hides their specific search. They will also discover how to delete specific sites from their search history.

2) Practical Parenting Tips for teens

a) Set up night time controls

There are many studies which show that teens who use their mobile phone at night in their bedroom lose out on several hours of sleep. Light from screens has long-been considered harmful to sleep patterns. The knock-on effects of a lack of sleep can result in a lack of attention in school, agitation, poor concentration levels and even depression.

It is therefore very important to introduce some sort of controls

over the use of your teenager's phone at night. Turning off the router can be effective in certain households but is not the answer for teens who use their data package on their phone to use the Internet at night.

A cut off time for the use of the phone should be established as soon as the child receives their first phone and this rule then becomes the norm into their teenage years (making it much easier to enforce).

b) The danger of listening to music at a high volume

Teens have only two settings when it comes to listening to music on their devices, off and full volume! As parents, it is our duty to constantly remind them that listening to music at a high-volume causes damage to their hearing and even eventual hearing loss. There are many studies out there which support these findings. Taking an eye break is also good for teens. In the US, it is recommended that every 20 minutes a person should take a 20 second break from the device screen and look at object 20 feet away, (known as the 20-20-20

rule)

c) The use of fake accounts to hurt others is illegal

While it is technically not illegal to set up a fake account, remind your child that it is illegal to use that fake account in a malicious way to hurt others. This topic is dealt with in more detail in chapter 6. Something that starts out as a bit of fun can be very stressful for the person on the receiving end and may lead to depression or even suicide.

d) Read permissions on all apps before downloading

This has been dealt with in more detail in chapter 4.
But just to recap on the main points:

- Check the user reviews of all apps – before installing them.
- All apps ask you for permission to access various features of your device. Always read the permissions list BEFORE installing an app.
- Keep your eyes and ears open for information on new apps trending at the moment.
- Talk to your children and make them aware of the dangers of harmful apps

e) Think twice before using Vault type apps

 We have discussed this topic in more detail in chapter 4 but just to recap on the main points:

- Remind your children of the dangers of taking and storing inappropriate images.
- Remind them that the sharing of sexually explicit images of anyone under the age of 17 is illegal.
- Get them to take a fresh look at the permissions that are needed to download certain apps and get them

thinking about who else may have access to all their 'private images' and what they can potentially do with them (based on the permission you gave them).

f) Set up a strong password to avoid Cyber Theft

The reasons why a secure password is essential and how to set up a strong password is dealt with in more detail in chapter 8, but the main measure that you need to communicate with your teen, is the need to have strong, secure passwords that are different for every account. Pass words need to be strong. Getting hacked is no fun! Most people tend to use the same password for multiple accounts so once a hacker discovers your weak password they often have access to many of your accounts. It's never too late to update the security on all of your devices and the mindset you have in relation to security.

g) Never click on a link without checking the URL.

Again, covered in chapter 6, a simple rule to remember is never click or open a link from anyone that you are not expecting. Your best friends email may have been hacked! I have seen this happen many times. Hover over the link to see where the URL takes you and in general be wary of all clickable links as they may well be malicious software that sits quietly on your device, without you even being aware that it is there, and mines information over a period of months!

Teach your children to ignore the flashing, scrolling ads and links that try to entice their clicks.

h) You are liable if your device is used by third parties

The onus is on you to keep your devices secure by using strong passwords. If your email address, website or social medial accounts are hacked and used to spread malicious material or spam, remember the ultimate responsibility lies with you! Never give your login credentials to anyone but close family. Remember, even relationships can fizzle out / come to an end and depending how they end, it could spell disaster for you if someone else can log in to your account.

i) Once you post something on the Internet, it is there forever

We need to constantly remind our children that everything that is posted on the internet is there forever! Never post anything that you would not let your granny read or look at! There are images that were once put up on Bebo (you might remember it - one of the  early Social Media platforms that is no longer available today), that can still be found on the Internet today. Try it for yourself by googling 'images from Bebo' and you will see just how easy it is to find all your old Bebo images from 10 years ago even though Bebo NO LONGER EXISTS!

What more proof does a teenager need that once you post something on the Internet, it is there FOREVER!!!

16 HOW TO...

Priest at wedding: "I now pronounce
husband and wife. You may now
update your Facebook status"

In this chapter, we will give you some tips, advice and some of the
steps that you will need in order to keep your child safe. We will also
look at setting up some of the more important controls that you need
to put in place.

1. How to Activate Parental Controls for YouTube Restricted Mode:

To implement the Parental Controls for YouTube, go to
YouTube.com and scroll down to the bottom of the page. You will
see a reference to Restricted Mode and it will say OFF. Click the Off
button, then click "On" and then click "Save". Adult content is now
filter out. Likewise, if you want to turn YouTube Restricted Mode Off,
reverse these simple steps.

Locking YouTube Restricted Mode:

As you will see, it's very easy to turn Restricted Mode on and off.
Therefore, you may want to lock it in order to ensure it is always
activated for all family members.

To Lock the Parental Control for YouTube, you will need a Google
account. To open a free Google account, go to google.com and click
"Sign In" in the top right-hand corner of their main website. You will
then see the option to create a new account.

Now return to YouTube and scroll down to the bottom of the page to the safety mode link as shown above.

After selecting the "On" button, you will see an option to Lock Restricted Mode ...

Select "Save and lock Restricted Mode on this browser". You will then be required to sign in to your Google account if you have not already done so.

Once Restricted Mode for YouTube video search is Locked, you can now log out of your account. Unlocking Restricted Mode on YouTube will require you to log into your account. This guarantees that no one else can deactivate the safety setting.

Important: If you have more than one browser on your computer, you will need to follow these steps for each browser.

2. How to check the device Browsing History

Every device comes with its own built in browser, however there is nothing stopping you from using a different browser – it is simply a matter of preference. Some browsers perform better on certain devices (e.g. Apple products always use the Safari Browser). I will briefly go through how to check the browsing history on each browser in turn. The steps are straightforward enough but if you do run into bother at any stage, simply google 'how to check the browser history' on your particular device for further help.

The 5 main browsers are as follows:

- Safari
- Chrome
- Internet Explorer
- Firefox
- Edge

Safari

First, open the Safari browser on your device. Next, click on Settings menu in the top right-hand corner of the screen. Scroll down until you locate the History option. When the drop-down menu appears your most recent history (generally the last 10 web pages that you have visited) will appear. Clicking on any of these items will take you directly to the respective page. Directly below it you will  find the rest of your recorded browsing history, grouped by day into sub-menus. If you have visited more than 10 web pages on the current day, there will also be a sub-menu present labelled "Earlier Today" containing the rest of today's history.

Google Chrome

Open your Google Chrome browser and click the Chrome menu on the browser toolbar. Again, this is located in the top right-hand corner of the screen (displayed as 3 dots stacked on top of each other). Select History from the drop down and the list of sites recently visited will be displayed. From there  you will be able to establish what sites were viewed, how often, at what time, etc

Internet Explorer

The History for Internet Explorer is accessed slightly differently to the first two browsers we have looked at. You will need to press the "ctrl" button and then tap the "H" button at the same time and the history will appear.

Firefox

Press the "alt" key on your keyboard and this will display the various Firefox menus across the top of the screen. Click on History and you will be able to choose from 'All History', 'Recently Closed Tabs', 'Recently Closed Windows'.

Edge

Click on the Hub icon ('3 dashes" next to the Star icon). Under History you can check all your previously visited sites.

If you discover something in the child's Browsing History that should not be there, then you will need to have a conversation about it with your child. Ask them why they felt the need to visit such a site and explain the dangers to them.

It also lets them know that you are keeping an eye on them and they will be less likely in the future to click on something they know they shouldn't, just out of curiosity.

Keep an open mind as they may well have accidently stumbled across an inappropriate site. There are so many pop ups and clickable links on certain sites that they are sometimes very difficult to avoid.

An example would be a website that offers the latest films 'for free' but bombards you with a whole host of sites that open automatically once you use it. These will appear in the device history even though you may have innocently set up the child on the couch to watch a nice film. Don't always blame the child!

Websites don't come with an appropriate age rating. Films released either in the Cinema or on DVD all come with a recommended age for which the particular film is appropriate. An eight-year-old child would never dream of trying to get into the cinema to watch an over 18's film. The age appropriate warning is usually enough of a deterrent and if that doesn't work, the staff are always there on hand to restrict access.

When you give a child a device which connects to the Internet, bear in mind that there are virtually no restrictions to stop them accessing all sorts of indecent material. It is up to you to put them in place and set the rules around what they can access and how long for.

As your child gets older, they will discover how to clear the browsing history. They will discover how to clear the full browsing history and how they can pick from the history and clear certain 'inappropriate' sites that they do not wish you to see. They also can clear everything looked at in the last hour, two hours, etc. Teens will also very quickly learn how to browse 'Incognito' which means they will not leave a search history behind them that you can check.

Probably the best way to deal with this issue is to restrict their ability to access certain websites / social media platforms via the home broadband router. In simple terms, the broadband entering your home passes through the Wi-Fi Router which broadcasts the Wi-Fi around the house. The router can be set up to act as a filter which won't allow access to certain sites (if set up correctly). How to set up your router correctly is dealt with in more detail in chapter 12 of this book.

3. Rules for downloading apps

Downloading apps is quite straightforward and most children, from a very young age, get the hang of it quite quickly. The problem for you is that your phone (or tablet) can end up with loads and loads of different games / apps; all of which are sitting there, taking up space, requiring updates, working away in the background, using up the battery and delivering alerts at the most inappropriate times.

My child once downloaded an app called 'Pou' which is exactly as it sounds, an animated lump of poo that you have to feed and keep happy. I quickly got rid of it as it used to make the most disgusting grunting sounds at the most inappropriate time of the day or night. Try explaining the grunting sound coming from the phone in your pocket to someone you are in conversation with!

That's when I decided enough was enough and we introduced some ground rules around the downloading of apps in our house. Rules are a very important tool in keeping your child safe so we have four basic rules as follows:

Rule 1: My younger children are simply not allowed to download an app unless they come to me first. This gives me a chance to read the permissions it requires, check the reviews, find out what the app does and make sure that it is age appropriate. If I come across an app that they have downloaded themselves without coming to me, they lose the device for a certain period of time. This generally works fine as everyone knows where they stand.

Rule 2: My older teens download apps themselves, but occasionally I will spot check their phones and have a look at the apps they are using. This means knowing their Pin to unlock the device (or whatever other security method they are using). They won't particularly like being spot checked and be prepared for some grief from them but as a parent you have to do what is best for them, even if they disagree! I also remind them to get into a habit of regularly checking the permissions. This makes them stop and think before making the decision as to whether they should allow an app to have access to all their personal data. For a more detailed look at dangerous apps, please read chapter 4.

Rule 3: Even if an app looks safe, particularly with younger children, I never download it unless we agree to delete one of the older apps that they no longer use. This is usually not an issue as kids get fed up with using some apps over time. It also helps clogging up your phone.

Rule 4: Once they have mastered the app, I would tend to sit with my child and get a tutorial from them. They are always eager and willing to show me how the app works and although I generally trust the reviews, it gives me the opportunity to check it out for myself. The app may have a feature that was not discussed in the reviews or not apparent in the description (e.g. a chatting or messaging facility that allows others to talk or chat directly with your child) As a parent, you need to make sure that it is suitable and appropriate for your child and there is no better way than playing the game or using the app yourself!

For the complete beginner, where can I download an app?

In order to download an app on to your device you will need to visit the Apple Store or the Play Store.
The Apple store is designed for IOS devices (generally anything created by Apple) and the Play Store is generally designed for Android Devices.

Most devices come pre-loaded with a clickable link or icon (usually located on the main screen) which will take you directly to the appropriate store for your device.

You may need to set up an account before you download anything from either store. You will be prompted if this is necessary. Follow the steps on screen but when you get to the step involving inputting your credit card details, check the small print to bypass this as you do not need your credit card linked to the store. The best way to avoid your children accidently or intentionally making a purchase on the store is by not having inputted your credit card details in the first place!

Once you have access to the store, you will be able to use the search facility to look for the apps that your kids want. There are also sections for 'most popular', 'top free', 'top selling', etc

There are thousands of free apps available however there are some apps that you simply have to purchase in order to download them. Apps make their money in different ways and the two most common ways are 'In-app purchases' and the other is advertising. The apps that you pay for are generally free from advertisements but you may have to make purchases within the game. These can add up over time.

Parents have to make up their own minds when it comes to the decision on whether to purchase an app or to go with the free version. I would always initially try the free version of a game if it is available and convince the child to put up with the ads in the short term as there is no guarantee that they will even like the game once they play it and it may well have been a waste of money if you purchased it straight away.

Remember to always read the permissions (i.e. what the app needs access to on your device), before downloading it and in general, the longer the list of permissions, the more you should be wary of it!

4. How to check your child's Social Media settings

Every Social Media platform can and should be set up in the best way possible in order to keep your child safe. I have showed you how to locate and set the proper settings in more detail in chapter 3. But always remember that no matter what Social Media platform your child is using, they all come with settings, restrictions and guidelines on how to use them properly. The recommended age for using each platform is just a guide and no-one knows your child better than you. Some are mature and responsible enough to handle most situations but the majority are not, so do bear this in mind when they are begging to be let on Facebook or Snapchat for the first time. Saying 'No' until you feel they are ready may be difficult at the time and not make you very popular but you are the parent and raising a child isn't a popularity contest!

5. How to run a Virus check on your device

In Chapter 8 ("**Scams, Malware & Password Security**") I gave you a recommendation for the type of Antivirus Software you should download and use. Now I will run through the steps involved in running an Antivirus check on your machine.

Kaspersky Free Antivirus Software is, in my opinion, the best on the market and comes highly recommended on several technology websites and magazines.

Once you have followed the simple steps for downloading, it will add an icon to your task bar. This will allow you to access it whenever necessary, set up your schedule and check the details of any threats detected.

If a threat is detected, you will be able to check the details of the threat by clicking on the 'Details' button shown above.

This will open up the notification centre and allow you to view the details (see below).

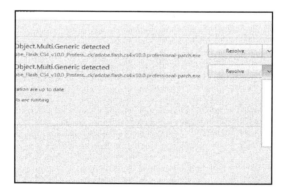

If you wish to set up a schedule to check your device for viruses, then you can do this through the settings section. The settings are represented by a cog located in the bottom left hand corner of the viewing panel.

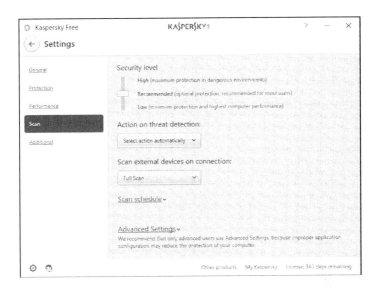

We recommend that a full scan takes place once a week. Select a day when the machine is not in full use, e.g. Sunday, as it may take an hour or even more to run a full check.

You could also schedule a quick scan to run daily and the settings will allow you to run the scan manually or automatically (either when your device starts, shuts down or at a time chosen by you, e.g. lunchtime).

6. How to set up a security lock on your phone or Tablet

Most devices, whether an IOS or an Android device, allow the user the ability to set up various levels of security on the device. A basic screen lock (a PIN, password, a pattern or fingerprint) is an effective way of preventing unrestricted access to your device. If your device doesn't already have a security lock of some sort, now is the time to do it. Phones and tablets can be passed around from child to child and the last thing you want is for someone else to be able to access personal data or your bank card details from last week's transactions!

To set up a screen lock on your device, go into the settings menu, represented by a cog and usually located in the top left-hand corner of the screen. On some devices, you may need to pull down the main menu from the top of the screen in order to see the settings option. Scroll through the options until you come across the Security heading. Click into this and follow the screen lock options. I would always recommend that you set up either a pattern, a PIN or a Password on your child's phone. Write the pattern, PIN or password down (ideally you could note it in Chapter 2 of this book titled 'My Details' and keep the book in a secure location) as you will be surprised how quickly you will forget it, even with the best will in the world.

Periodically check the device security to make sure your child hasn't figured out how to change it for themselves. There are a whole host of security settings that you can and should investigate under the security settings on each of the devices in your home (e.g. you can set another PIN to prevent your child from making calls. This is a separate PIN to unlocking the device to play games).

My advice is that you the parent should stay in control of the device security at all times. Rules create boundaries for children and children need to know where the boundaries lie and who is in control of them. If they misbehave, you have the option of re-setting the security on their device in order to limit or prevent access for a set period of time.

7. How to create a strong password

Please refer to Chapter 8 for details on the best practice for creating passwords.

8. How to setup email accounts on your device:

As you would expect, Google have made it very easy to set up Gmail through an Android phone or tablet. To setup your Gmail on an Android phone, follow these steps.

1. Open the Settings menu and go to Accounts & sync settings on your device.
2. The Accounts & sync settings screen displays your current sync settings and a list of your current accounts.
3. Touch Add account.
4. Touch Google to add your Google Apps account.
5. Touch Sign in when prompted for your Google Account.
6. Enter your full Google Apps email address as your username, and then enter your password.
7. Select which services you'd like to sync.

To setup email on your Apple device is well documented and the easiest suggestion I have for you is to use google to find relevant articles for your particular model.

CONCLUSION

Spending a day on Facebook has once again fooled me into believing I have an actual social life!

A parent once described the Internet to me in very simple terms. In his opinion, the Internet was like a big city; it has good areas and bad areas, some great things to see and some horrific sights that no-one should ever see. In general, it is full of good people but also has some nasty characters with whom you don't want to be acquainted.

You wouldn't abandon your child in the heart of a big city, would you? In effect, that is what you are doing every time you let your kids use the Internet unsupervised!

We are too quick to allow our kids to play in the biggest, most dangerous playground humanity has ever created – the Internet.

I believe it boils down to some good, old fashioned parenting techniques mentioned throughout the earlier chapters:

- **Know what your kids are getting up to** - whenever they are using the Internet.
- **Talk to your kids regularly** – find out what games they play, apps they download, who they follow, what they watch.
- **Restrict access at certain times** – whether it's to ensure they get a good night's sleep, whether you deem a certain platform or game to be age inappropriate or if it is simply one of the punishments you dish out.
- **Set the ground rules** – Keep the Internet out of the bedroom

and use the tools available to you to monitor online activity and remove access to inappropriate content.

- **Monitor their online activity** – watch for mood changes, temper tantrums, general changes in behaviour when they use the internet.
- Remember, **You're the Boss**! – both parents should sing from the same hymn sheet and stand firm whenever you say 'No'

If you follow these basic rules, I am confident that the world will be a safer place. No-one expects you to be an expert. No-one expects you to even try to match what your kids know. As a parent, you will have to have those fights, and you will more often than not think (and endure being told) that your kids hate you. Here's the truth about parenting: if you give your kids the safe environment that they need; if you give them boundaries and limits and teach them the simple moral truths that you were taught by your parents, eventually they will grow up to not hate you and might eventually become your friends. Just remember, you only have one responsibility – to get your kids to adulthood safely!

INDEX

A

B

C

D

T

U

V

W

Y

LINKS & REFERENCES

We hope that you will find the following links and references useful. For clickable versions of these links, please go to the following webpage:

www.schoolswebsites.ie/pages/istlinks.php

Important Resources

1. **YouTube: "CEOP Channel"**
   Child Exploitation and Online Protection Centre

2. www.Nobullying.com

3. www.watchyourspace.ie

4. www.webopedia.com/quick_ref/textmessageabbreviations.asp

5. www.Hotline.ie

6. **The Garda National Crime Prevention Unit,**
   Garda H.Q., Harcourt Square, Dublin 2.
   Tel: (01) 6663362, Fax: (01) 6663314
   Email: crime_prevention@garda.ie
   www.garda.ie

7. **Office for Internet Safety**
   www.internetsafety.ie

8. **Child Safety Issues**
   www.childline.ie

9. **Website of National Parents Council**
   www.npc.ie

10. <u>Tips on Internet Safety</u>
www.webwise.ie

11. <u>**Irish hotline for public to report child pornography and other illegal content on the internet**</u>
www.hotline.ie

12. <u>Video Tutorials</u>
   - **Think before you share** - www.educatorstechnology.com/2016/09/5-excellent-video-tutorials-to-teach.html
   - **Protect your stuff** - www.youtube.com/watch?v=ue1r_63GkIw
   - **Know & use your settings** - www.youtube.com/watch?v=ALJk5416mNM
   - **Avoid scams** - www.youtube.com/watch?v=BX3y_an89PQ
   - **Be positive** - www.youtube.com/watch?v=5XXlDS7TtwY

13. <u>A helpline for Parents</u> - offers support, guidance and information on all aspects of being a parent
www.parentline.ie/

14. <u>**Simple safety advice from Google**</u>
www.google.com/safetycenter/tools/

Useful Resources

1. **Windows Family Safety:** familysafety.microsoft.com

2. **AVG Family Safety:** www.avg.com/us-en/avg-family-safety

3. **K9 Web Protection browser:**

iTunes: itunes.apple.com/app/k9-web-protection-browser/id407657840
Android:
play.google.com/store/apps/details?id=com.k99k5.k9browser

4. **McGruff Safe Guard Mobile Browser:**
itunes.apple.com/us/app/mcgruff-safeguard-browser/id493861295?mt=8

5. **MobSafety Ranger Browser:**
iTunes: itunes.apple.com/us/app/ranger-browser-safe-internet/id406480823?mt=8
Android:
play.google.com/store/apps/details?id=com.gpit.android.safe.Ranger&hl=en

6. **Restricted Profiles:** www.pcadvisor.co.uk/how-to/google-android/3461359/parental-control-on-android/

7. **Blocking Advertisements on Browsers:**
dottech.org/17516/block-ads-in-firefox-internet-explorer-chrome-and-opera-how-to/

8. **Gmail:**
Android:
play.google.com/store/apps/details?id=com.google.android.gm&hl=en
iTunes: itunes.apple.com/app/gmail/id422689480

9. How **to setup email accounts on your Apple device:**
www.gilsmethod.com/how-to-setup-email-accounts-on-the-ipad

10. **Facebook Privacy:**
www.facebook.com/help/445588775451827

11. **Email Scams:**
www.wikihow.com/Spot-an-Email-Hoax-or-Phishing-Scam

12. YouTube Parental Controls:
www.youtube.com/watch?feature=player_embedded&v=gkI3 e0P3S5E

13. Guide to abbreviated Text Messages:
www.webopedia.com/quick_ref/textmessageabbreviations.asp

References

All references to external sources used in the book are listed here:

1. Netflix; Black Mirror, "Shut Up and Dance" (imdb.com) 2016
2. Tracking WannaCry BitCoin payments: Keith Collins; Twitter handle: @collinskeith
3. "predator". The American Heritage® Science Dictionary. Houghton Mifflin Company. 28 Jul. 2017.
4. en.wikipedia.org/wiki/The_Ryan_Tubridy_Show
5. www.rte.ie/news/player/prime-time/2014/1204/
6. www.urbandictionary.com/define.php?term=Catfishing
7. "Catching Creeps" on YouTube: www.youtube.com/results?search_query=catching+creeps
8. "Omegle Child Predator" on YouTube: www.youtube.com/watch?v=-okd7FzPzFI
9. Facebook can track you: www.independent.co.uk/life-style/gadgets-and-tech/news/facebook-know-smartphones-activity-what-do-not-use-social-network-account-media-privacy-security-a7892761.html
10. Google can track you: www.avclub.com/article/google-has-found-way-track-you-even-when-youre-not-255875
11. AI predicting time of death: www.globalfuturist.org/2017/06/an-australian-ai-can-predict-when-youll-die-with-70-percent-accuracy/
12. AI spotting extremist posts: www.nytimes.com/2017/06/15/technology/facebook-artificial-intelligence-extremists-terrorism.html?_r=0
13. AI composing music: flipboard.com/@flipboard/-this-ai-powered-robot-can-play-the-mari/f-bd7f3d05f1%2Ftheverge.com
14. Tristan Harris on Social Media; Ted Talk 2017; www.ted.com/talks/tristan_harris_the_manipulative_tricks_te

ch_companies_use_to_capture_your_attention

15. Origins of the Internet: J.C.R. Licklider & W. Clark, "On-Line Man Computer Communication", August 1962

16. Origins of the Internet: L. Roberts & T. Merrill, "Toward a Cooperative Network of Time-Shared Computers", Fall AFIPS Conf., Oct. 1966

17. Arpanet: L. Roberts, "Multiple Computer Networks and Intercomputer Communication", ACM Gatlinburg Conf., October 1967

18. WORLD INTERNET USAGE AND POPULATION STATISTICS MARCH 31, 2017 (www.internetworldstats.com)

19. The Internet of Things: Internet of Things (IoT) History (www.postscapes.com)

20. The Internet Of Things (www.forbes.com)

21. "deindividuation"; Wikipedia (en.wikipedia.org/wiki/Deindividuation)

22. Everybody lies: William Belle, OYE Times, 2011 (www.oyetimes.com)

23. "Trolling" - Urban Dictionary (www.urbandictionary.com)

24. Bullying Prevention for Schools: A Step-by-Step Guide to Implementing a Successful Anti-Bullying Program, by Allan L. Beane, Ph.D.; Jossey-Bass, 2009

25. "Social Media"; Merriam-Webster (www.merriam-webster.com/dictionary/social media)

26. Social Media statistics: Priit Kallas,Top 15 Most Popular Social Networking Site and Apps, July 2017 (www.dreamgrow.com)

27. SnapChat safety: www.snapchat.com/safety/

28. SnapChat tips: support.snapchat.com/en-US/a/safety-tips-resources

29. SnapChat guidelines: support.snapchat.com/en-US/a/guidelines

30. SnapChat settings: support.snapchat.com/en-US/a/privacy-settings

31. SnapChat: support.snapchat.com/a/find-friends-map

32. SnapChat: support.snapchat.com/a/location-snap-map

33. SnapChat: support.snapchat.com/en-US/a/block-friends

34. SnapChat: support.snapchat.com/en-US/i-need-help

35. YouTube: support.google.com/youtube

36. YouTube:
    support.google.com/youtube/topic/2676378?hl=en&ref_topi
    c= 6151248
37. YouTube:
    support.google.com/youtube/topic/2946312?hl=en&ref_topi
    c= 2803240
38. YouTube:
    support.google.com/youtube/topic/2946312?hl=en&ref_topi
    c= 2803240
39. Instagram bought by Facebook:
    help.instagram.com/155833707900388
40. Instagram:
    help.instagram.com/116024195217477/?helpref=hc_fnav
41. Instagram Community Guidelines:
    help.instagram.com/477434105621119/?helpref=hc_fnav
42. Instagram Help: help.instagram.com
43. Instagram support:
    help.instagram.com/426700567389543/?helpref=hc_fnav
44. WhatsApp usage: blog.whatsapp.com/616/One-billion
45. WhatsApp:
    www.facebook.com/jan.koum/posts/10152994719980011
46. WhatsApp: blog.whatsapp.com/10000618/end-to-end-
    encryption
47. WhatsApp: Romain Aubert, Why I Told my Friends to stop
    using WhatsApp and Telegram, (freecodecamp.org), January,
    2017
48. MetaData mining: www.eff.org/deeplinks/2013/06/why-
    metadata-matters
49. WhatsApp threats: James Frew, 4 Security Threats WhatsApp
    Users Need Know (makeuseof.com), March 2017
50. Philip Bates, How a Minor Data Breach Made Headline News
    & Ruined Reputations (makeuseof.com), November 2014
51. Signal: whispersystems.org
52. WhatsApp guide: faq.whatsapp.com/en/general/21197244
53. Google Images: Search for images with Reverse image search
    (support.google.com)
54. Facebook policy: www.facebook.com/policy.php
55. Facebook help: www.facebook.com/help.php?page=419
56. Facebook settings: www.facebook.com/settings?tab=account

57. Facebook settings:
www.facebook.com/*nameofpage*/settings/?tab=settings

58. musical.ly/en-US/for-parents

59. musical.ly guidelines: musical.ly/en-US/community-guidelines

60. Yellow guidelines: community.yellw.co

61. Children producing porn: Jamie Bartlett, The Dark Net: Inside the Digital Underworld (William Heinemann: London), 2014

62. Omegle: www.omegle.com/static/privacy.html

63. YouTube mind reader:
www.youtube.com/watch?v=F7pYHN9iC9I

64. Instagram image ownership: help.instagram.com

65. Cyberbullying - laws: cyberbullying.org/cyberbullying-laws

66. Cyberbullying defined: www.cyberbullying.org

67. Cyberbullying statistics: www.ispcc.ie/file/7/19_0/Bullying+-+the+facts.pdf

68. Home used to be a refuge: www.nobullying.com/examination-of-cyber-bullying- in-ireland

69. Ikydz router: (www.ikydz.com)

70. How to setup email accounts on your Apple device:
www.gilsmethod.com/how-to-setup-email-accounts-on-the-ipad

71. Total number of apps worldwide:
www.statista.com/statistics/.../number-of-apps-available-in-leading-app-stores/

72. Google apps statistics: www.quora.com/How-many- new-apps- are-added- to-Google-Play- everyday

73. Ikydz router: www.ikydz.com

DEVICE DETAILS

Use this section to record the information you need to manage your home IT equipment, Internet and Wifi access. Once you've recorded information here – keep this book secure and DON'T LET YOUR KIDS SEE IT!

DEVICE #1 DETAILS

Make: _____

Model: _____

Serial Number: _____

Login Username: _____

Login Password: _____

PIN (if applicable): _____

Other Details:

DEVICE #2 DETAILS

Make: _____

Model: _____

Serial Number: _____

Login Username: _____

Login Password: _____

PIN (if applicable): _____

Other Details:

DEVICE #3 DETAILS

Make: _____

Model: _____

Serial Number: _____

Login Username: _____

Login Password: _____

PIN (if applicable): _____

Other Details:

DEVICE #4 DETAILS

Make: _____

Model: _____

Serial Number: _____

Login Username: _____

Login Password: _____

PIN (if applicable): _____

Other Details:

DEVICE #5 DETAILS

Make: _____

Model: _____

Serial Number: _____

Login Username: _____

Login Password: _____

PIN (if applicable): _____

Other Details:

DEVICE #6 DETAILS

Make: _____

Model: _____

Serial Number: _____

Login Username: _____

Login Password: _____

PIN (if applicable): _____

Other Details:

DEVICE #7 DETAILS

Make: _____

Model: _____

Serial Number: _____

Login Username: _____

Login Password: _____

PIN (if applicable): _____

Other Details:

DEVICE #8 DETAILS

Make: _____

Model: _____

Serial Number: _____

Login Username: _____

Login Password: _____

PIN (if applicable): _____

Other Details:

DEVICE #9 DETAILS

Make: _____

Model: _____

Serial Number: _____

Login Username: _____

Login Password: _____

PIN (if applicable): _____

Other Details:

DEVICE #10 DETAILS

Make: _____

Model: _____

Serial Number: _____

Login Username: _____

Login Password: _____

PIN (if applicable): _____

Other Details:

ABOUT THE AUTHORS

J Pagden

Mr. Pagden comes from a family of educators, and is himself a qualified secondary school teacher by profession, with a passion for all things technological. He has spent the last 4 years of his professional life travelling the roads of Ireland to hundreds of primary and secondary schools across the country, speaking to everyone (children, students, teachers and parents) about the need for a heightened understanding of the inherent dangers of the Internet.

He lives in Galway on the west coast of Ireland with his wife, two children (his son is at university while his daughter is a rebellious 17-year-old) and their most-loved cocker spaniel – Spud.

D Moran

Mr. Moran has spent the last 25 years of his working life in various Management and Quality roles both here in Ireland and abroad. For the last 10 years he has worked very closely with the Irish Education sector and has helped to develop a number of software solutions currently used in hundreds of schools here in Ireland. He shares a passion for Internet Safety along with his Business Partner Mr Pagden.

He lives along the Wild Atlantic Way in Co Mayo with his wife and four children, ranging in ages from 8 years of age up to the age of 16 and is patiently waiting for a visit from Sam Maguire!

Praise for the Internet Safety Talks in Schools

Below are a selection of just some of the testimonials received from various schools throughout the country (Primary and Post Primary).

Testimonial from Anne-Marie Farrell - Principal of Ballaghlea NS, Co. Galway

"Lurtel Ltd.'s, Mr. Pagden came to our school to deliver internet safety training talks to pupils and parents recently. The content was very current and relative to each audience which is important in the ever-changing environment of technology. Pupils were extremely engaged in the workshop and responded very well to the follow up activities. Parents were given very useful tips on how to protect their children. They were also given the knowledge on how to make better choices for their children, when accessing and using the internet. The training was a very worthwhile exercise and I would highly recommend it to other schools and clubs."

Testimonial from John Conlon Principal St. Clare's P.S. Manorhamilton, Co Leitrim

I would highly recommend Lurtel – Cyberbullying & Internet Safety Workshop to other schools primary or secondary, I think it is an essential for teachers or parents. We invited every household from 3rd to 6th class and had almost 90 parents in attendance. Mr. Pagden did a full 2 hours for the staff and 2 hours 20minutes with parents and covered everything, answered all questions. He was really passionate about the topic, had everyone spellbound but did not frighten or over emphasise the dangers. The only negative feedback I got was that it could have longer as you could listen to Mr. Pagden all day. He gave excellent advice and was completely practical. The follow up activities were perfect to bed down the understanding. The feedback from children, parents and teachers has been unprecedented in its positivity. Mr. Pagden was equally good with the children as with the adults and had tailored presentations for each group.

I wish everything would work as well.

Testimonial from Norma O'Brien, Principal Coláiste Mhuire, Askeaton, Co. Limerick

"Mr Pagden delivered two days of Internet Safety presentations to our school community. His style and delivery were excellent and expertly pitched for the different age groups. Students, parents and teachers found the content accessible and informative. This is a difficult topic but a 'must' for all schools. I am very happy to recommend Mr Pagden, it was a very positive experience for our school".

Testimonial from Amanda Rice, ICT Coordinator, Colaiste Phobail Rosrea

"Mr. Pagden was excellent and had an excellent way with students".

Testimonial from Anna Maria Newell, SPHE Coordinator, Presentation College Athenry

"The feedback from staff and students was very positive. The students were very attentive all throughout his 90-minute talk and the staff members who were present found his presentation very interesting and engaging. I would definitely recommend him to other schools for students, staff and parents. We would hope to have him back to deliver his presentation to other year groups in the future".

Testimonial from a parent from CBS Thurles, Co Tipperary

" I have been to lots of these talks over the last few years and Mr. Pagden's was by far the best I ever attended"

Testimonial from Tim Coffey Deputy Principal from CBS Thurles, Co Tipperary

"Brilliant talk! The way it was explained was excellent. Well done to all"

Testimonial from Elaine, Parents Association, Carrowholly NS

"The topics covered were relevant and presented in a very positive and informative manner. The use of practical examples of real life scenarios, made it easy to understand the potential risks that exist for our children on the internet, mobile phones and tablets.

More importantly, we were given incredibly useful tips that we as parents can use to help protect our children. After completing the training, I felt empowered and more confident to make better choices to keep my children safe while they are using the different technologies available to them. Would highly recommend this course - an invaluable resource for all parents".

Testimonial from Peter Carney, Principal Carrowholly NS

"Just a note to say thanks very much to yourself and Mr. Pagden for hosting the Internet Safety/Cyber Bullying course yesterday 24th November 2015 in the school.

The feedback has been great from both the children who attended during school and the parents who attended in the evening.

The course content and presentation skills are really excellent, making it interesting to listen to and also very informative with many practical tips to help protect our children and ourselves on the internet/ social media sites".

Testimonial from Joe Kennelly, Principal - Cregmore NS

"It was the most worthwhile hour and a half investment we have spent in the school in a long time and I urge every school to participate in the seminar."

Testimonial from Gillian Broderick, PA - Brackloon NS

"'Thank You' to yourself and Mr. Pagden for the excellent workshops you provided for the children and parents at our school last Monday. The children have been doing plenty of talking about the topics discussed, and it has definitely heightened their awareness of the dangers of the Internet.

So many parents have commented to me during the week that they found the talk really informative, and very worthwhile, and needless to say a bit scary!

I would certainly highly recommend this program for anyone with children. I hope you two are kept busy delivering it, as it has to have a positive impact on children.

Testimonial from Marie O'Donnell, Principal - Bangor NS

The kids talk and parents talk was absolutely excellent. Mr Pagden's delivery was superb. He truly deserves credit for his wonderful ability to clearly deliver on what is a complex issue. I am recommending it to my own children's school, Glencastle NS and to the local secondary schools, St. Brendan's College Belmullet and Our Lady's Belmullet.

Testimonial from Bernadette Ryan, Principal Holy Family NS

"Mr. Pagden delivered Internet Safety training to 4th, 5th and 6th class in our school. Both children and teachers found it very informative and interesting! The parents really enjoyed the Internet Safety talk and suggested having the talk every year! We will definitely have Lurtel back again"

Testimonial from Michael Carney, Principal, Myna NS

"Members of the Lurtel team gave internet safety talks to the children in 3rd, 4th, 5th and 6th in our school recently. They were informative, interesting, very well presented and pitched perfectly for the children attending the power point presentations. I would recommend all schools to run the programme".

Testimonial from Karen Franklin, Principal Nicker NS, Co. Limerick

"Thank you to Lurtel Ltd (Mr. Moran and Mr. Pagden) for your time and expertise. All parents really enjoyed the sessions and found the information very helpful. I know the children benefitted greatly from same, as did their teachers".

Testimonial from Mary Dunlea, Principal St Tola's NS, Shannon

"I highly recommend the workshops on Internet safety for both pupils and parents. They were delivered in an informative and professional manner and the pupils learnt a lot.

I will also recommend the workshops to our neighbouring schools. They provide a very valuable service and I'm delighted that the parents found it to be worthwhile also".

Parent from St. Michael's Primary School, Trim Co Meath

"I've been to lots of talks and this was by far the best one I have ever been to"

Parent from Scoil Muire Agus Padraig, Swinford Co Mayo

"The training session with Mr. Pagden was excellent and very informative. The information I was given, I found to be useful as I am only learning about this world through my daughters. I didn't know I could turn off the router at night or change passwords. This gives me great control. I would recommend this training to other parents."

Testimonial from Irene Gielty, Principal Dooagh NS, Co Mayo

"We wish to extend our sincere thanks to Mr. Pagden from Lurtel for an extremely informative and worthwhile talk for our parents on Internet Safety and Cyber-Bullying. He also conducted a workshop on the same topics with the children from 3rd to 6th Class, presenting the information in an effective manner - the children were totally engaged for 2 hours and learned so much. We would highly recommend this talk/workshop for both children and parents. We consider it probably the best money we have spent this year"

Testimonial from Bernie, a teacher from Carraigin Rua NS, Boyle

" Best talk I have ever been to!"

Testimonial from Vanessa Fairweather, Principal Tierneevin NS

"Thank you on behalf of our pupils, staff and parents for the seminars which were so relevant and up to date and pitched, in my opinion, at just the right level for the children. It is fair to say that everybody went home having learnt something".

Testimonial from Peter Walsh, Principal St Conaires NS, Shannon

"In recent years, teachers have seen the vital role that technology plays in the classroom. It can tend to the varying needs of all children in a highly motivating and engaging manner. However, technology can equally have as much a negative impact on school children as a positive. This external influence has now become an integral part in children's lives. Unfortunately, young people are using their phones and computer devices without having the necessary skills and understanding to fully comprehend how a certain website can negatively impact on their lives. Cyber-bullying and exposure to inappropriate material are now issues that educators must deal with in the classroom every day. It would be impossible to deter children from using this technology but rather we should come to understand it ourselves first and then pass this knowledge to the children. For this reason, Mr. Pagden was invited to speak to both the staff and some of the student body in our school. He provided real life examples of how this powerful resource can be misused by some people for the wrong reasons. Step-by-step he showed the students how simple it is for strangers to gain private and personal information and images from their accounts. It soon became clear the prior beliefs the children had about their competency with using computers and social media were misguided. The children and the staff were left shocked by Mr. Pagden's clear and relevant examples. His presentation was informative, engaging and insightful. Future approaches to the use of technology have been influenced greatly by Mr. Pagden's presentation".

Testimonial from Sally O Neill, Principal St Sennan's NS, Clare

"The highlight of Internet Safety Day was the workshop carried out with the children in the senior classes of the school.

They were immediately engaged by the facilitator and learned necessary lessons about being safe on social media. The impact of this learning also fell on our parents who willingly attended the Parents evening. Every part of that workshop was valuable and parents went home a little more confident that they could deal with the challenges of social media rather than ignore the potential dangers."

Testimonial from Martin McCabe, 2nd Year Head, Colaiste Na Hinse, Bettystown, Co. Meath

"Thank you for facilitating the talks for our 1st and 2nd year students. All students and staff have responded very positively in relation to the subject matter and presentation of talks. On the latter, Mr. Pagden is one of the best guest speakers I have had the pleasure of listening to. His calm yet controlled approach ensured that all students listened intently and yet felt comfortable enough to ask questions and interact throughout. In my entire teaching career, I have never witnessed anyone who is able to engage an entire year group of 2nd year students the way Mr. Pagden did"

Testimonial from John McNally Counsellor and Psychotherapist, Thurles, Co Tipperary

" I attended this talk in June 2016, delivered by Lurtel LTD. on Cyber Bullying and Internet Safety. I work with victims of bullying, sexual abuse and suicidal teens and adults many of whom suffer the effects of these internet abuses. It was very informative, very clearly delivered, and the message was made very clear......"
Internet beware, put safety first " it was a superb delivery by a very knowledgeable company "

Testimonial from Hazel Cosgrove, Principal Culmore NS, Co Mayo

" We were greatly impressed with the presentation to both students and parents on Internet Safety & Cyber Bullying. Mr. Pagden's presentation to children was age appropriate and he managed to create a very relaxed atmosphere, where the children were able to talk freely about any issues. Equally, the parents training session was full of excellent information and advice on how to keep their children safe on the internet. This was a very worthwhile investment in the safety of our children and should be mandatory in every school".

Testimonial from Marian Kitson, Principal Kilmaine NS, Co Mayo

" Our school recently engaged the services of Lurtel to provide Internet Safety talks for our pupils and also for our parent body. I cannot recommend Lurtel highly enough. From the moment we contacted Declan, nothing was a problem. He was so accommodating and helpful. Mr. Pagden is an excellent speaker and really gained the children's attention and more importantly their trust. The children accepted and heeded his words of guidance far more readily that they would from us as teachers. Parents were delighted with Mr. Pagden's very comprehensive talk and I was impressed with how generous he was with his time. No-one felt rushed and all areas of concern were addressed.

This was our first year conducting formal internet safety talks but we will certainly be incorporating them into our school calendar going forward".

Parent from Taugheen NS, Co Mayo

"I am a mother from Taugheen National School who attended your information meeting Monday night last. I found the session to be extremely informative but most importantly I felt it gave me control back. I now know where to start in order to make the devices in our home safer and it has me more aware of what my children could be doing on the internet and what threats these may cause. It was extremely well given and all points were very relevant. I would and have already highly recommended this training evening for anyone who is lucky enough to be able to avail of it. Many thanks."

Testimonial from Nuala Gallagher, Principal Killenumery NS, Co Leitrim

"While the internet has provided so many advantages, a number of less than pleasant disadvantages present themselves. We all agree that the internet is for the most part a safe environment for all but as teachers, parents and children we need to know how to navigate it in a safe and secure way for all concerned. As a school community we were given extremely useful tips to do this. Our understanding of the very real and possible risks that exist was heightened. I highly recommend this talk to school communities. The content and its presentation were excellent. Many thanks".

Testimonial from Anna Maher, Principal Castleblakeney NS, Co Galway

"We at Castleblakeney National School were impressed with the Internet Safety Presentation given by Lurtel to both our students, their parents and staff. Mr. Pagden covered internet concerns along with the dangerous and difficult situations that can arise from using mobile phones and other technology. He used actual cases to alert all of us to the dangers of posting on social media and made us realise it could happen to us. Mr. Pagden made parents more aware of their children's time spent on technology and how easy it is to fail to protect them.

The presentation was real, relevant and quite alarming. We would recommend Lurtel as an excellent provider for Internet Safety and Cyber Bullying Training to any organisation".

Made in the USA
Columbia, SC
01 October 2017